M000190787

# ARCHAEOLOGY, RITUAL, RELIGION

The archaeology of religion is a much neglected area, yet religious sites and artefacts constitute a major area of archaeological evidence. Timothy Insoll here presents an introductory statement on the archaeology of religion, examining what archaeology can tell us about religion, the problems of defining and theorising religion in archaeology, and the methodology, or how to 'do', the archaeology of religion.

This volume assesses religion and ritual through a range of examples from around the world and across time, including pre-historic religions, shamanism, African religions, death, landscape, and even food. Insoll also discusses the history of research and varying theories in this field before looking to future research directions. This book is a valuable guide for students and archaeologists, and initiate a major debate.

**Timothy Insoll** is Lecturer in Archaeology at the School of Art History and Archaeology of the University of Manchester. His previous publications include *The Archaeology of Islam* (1999), *Archaeology and World Religion* (2001) and *The Archaeology of Islam in Sub-Saharan Africa* (2003).

# THEMES IN ARCHAEOLOGY
## Edited by Julian Thomas
*University of Manchester*

## THE ARCHAEOLOGY OF PERSONHOOD
*An anthropological approach*
Chris Fowler

## ARCHAEOLOGY, RITUAL, RELIGION
Timothy Insoll

# ARCHAEOLOGY, RITUAL, RELIGION

*Timothy Insoll*

LONDON AND NEW YORK

First published 2004
by Routledge
2 Park Square, Milton Park, Abingdon, Oxon OX14 4RN

Simultaneously published in the USA and Canada
by Routledge
270 Madison Ave, New York, NY 10016

Reprinted 2005

Transferred to Digital Printing 2007

*Routledge is an imprint of the Taylor & Francis Group, an informa business*

© 2004 Timothy Insoll

Typeset in Garamond by BC Typesetting Ltd, Bristol
Printed and bound in Great Britain by
TJI Digital, Padstow, Cornwall

*British Library Cataloguing in Publication Data*
A catalogue record for this book is available from the British Library

*Library of Congress Cataloging in Publication Data*
A catalog record for this book has been requested

ISBN 10: 0-415-25312-8 (hbk)
ISBN 10: 0-415-25313-6 (pbk)

ISBN 13: 978-0-415-25312-3 (hbk)
ISBN 13: 978-0-415-25313-0 (pbk)

In memory of David Turner (1966–2000)

# CONTENTS

# FIGURES

# ACKNOWLEDGEMENTS

First, I would like to thank Rachel MacLean and Julian Thomas for commenting on the text. I would also like to thank Rachel and Freya for allowing me the time to write this book. Sekou Berthe and Modibo Diallo are likewise gratefully acknowledged for accompanying me from Bamako to Bobo and onto Dafra. Acknowledgement is also due to the peaceful surroundings of the K.R.Cama Oriental Research Institute Library in Bombay where in an afternoon during the monsoon, frameworks began to coalesce. The Gten Photographic Unit at the University of Manchester are also thanked for their usual exemplary standards of service.

I am also grateful to Professor Frank Willett for providing illustrations from his excavations at Ife, Nigeria, to Paul Bahn and Marek Zvelebil for supplying offprints, and to Mark White for answering a prehistory query. Acknowledgement is also due to Peter Mitchell, Chris Evans, and Eleanor Casella for providing references. Obviously, all the responsibility for the content, errors, and shortcomings of this volume remains my own. I would also like to thank Jan Dixon for supplying Inter-Library loan vouchers, and Chris Fowler for having an ever-interesting bookshelf. Finally, gratitude is also extended to the participants of the Manchester Conference on Archaeology and Religions for much interesting debate, and similarly to the various cohorts of students who have completed my MA option, The Archaeology of Religions.

*Figure 1* View of Dafra (photo T. Insoll)

# PROLOGUE

Our Malian assistant, Modibo, was told to remove his red shirt, this being a forbidden colour in the shrine, he did this and placed it on a specific rock indicated by the priest. The priest knocked three times on trees, twice to introduce us to the shrine as we descended into the gorge in which it is located. Clogged with tall trees interlaced with creepers, this gorge formed an anomalous feature in the otherwise arid landscape, a sense of difference reinforced by the striking contrast in light from the glare encountered in the plain above to that of the dappled shade of the sacred forest.

On entering the forest our attention was immediately drawn to a large hearth indicated by three blackened stones and a circle of ash surrounded for several metres by a mass of feathers (Figure 1). Here the priest halted and checked that everything required for the ritual was present – chickens, and a handful of ash. He and everyone else took off their shoes, and the party proceeded a further 60 metres to the shrine which itself does not become visible until about 10 metres distant. Then hidden under a mass of creepers and hanging vegetation the 'holy of holies' is seen: a large free-standing boulder, 2 metres in height and about a metre in width, smeared with blood and shea butter and close to, but not touching, one of the walls of the gorge. Some 5 metres from the shrine is a large pool fed by a stream entering the gorge and in turn feeding a further smaller pool downstream.

Each participant is either handed a live chicken or, if holding one already, upside down as instructed, is told to communicate their desires to the god(s) silently whilst the chicken is in their hands. The chicken is then passed to the priest who plucks a single long feather from its wing and inserts it vertically into a mass of congealed blood which sits on top of the shrine. The chicken's throat is then cut by the priest, and the blood drained onto this feather. Whether the sacrifice has been accepted is also checked by the priest through throwing the chicken down to the left-hand side of the shrine. If it lies still it is inauspicious, if it flutters vigorously while dying this is a good sign. The priest next questions, in the presence of the shrine, each of the participants as to what they will sacrifice here as an act of gratitude should their desires be fulfilled (cattle, horses, camels, guinea fowl, sheep, goats, pig, but not dog or donkey, were all described as permissible sacrifices). The chickens were then collected from where they lay and the priest led the way back to the fireplace.

At the fireplace the priest gathered together a few handfuls of dry brushwood and leaves and started a fire. This done, he soaked the chicken briefly in the adjacent stream before lightly singeing the carcass to assist in burning off some of the feathers, others being plucked by hand. The ribcage was then broken open and the entrails removed and cleaned; the carcass minus the entrails was put to one side to be kept by the priest. Our group, led by the priest, then returned to the upper pool next to the shrine. Here, the priest summoned to the surface the sacred catfish which inhabit the pool with a repeated monotonous call which echoed off the surrounding rocks. Overhead a group of vultures watched the proceedings from the trees. The catfish, giants, broke the surface of the pool with their mouths and were rewarded by the priest with small pieces of the chicken entrails fed by hand. This achieved, a portion of entrails was reserved and the same ritual repeated at the second pool downstream, where the catfish were noticeably smaller.

The feeding of the catfish complete, we returned to the shrine where the priest took some of the shea butter smeared on the shrine and rubbed it on each of the participant's hands. Each was advised not to wash their hands using hot water for the next 24 hours. The ritual was concluded.

This is an impressionistic description of a sacrificial ritual completed in January 2002 at Dafra, *c*. 8 km south-east of the town of Bobo-Dioulasso in Burkina Faso. How would we retrieve this as archaeologists? The issues which underlie this seemingly simple question are the focus of this book, and later we shall return to this problem in relation to Dafra itself.

# 1

# INTRODUCTION TO
# THE THEME

## The theme

Although potentially a vast topic, the archaeology of religion is
in fact substantially neglected as regards the provision of a convenient and accessible introductory text, and this volume aims to
redress this. Nevertheless, pretensions are not entertained here
that what is provided is the definitive statement on the relationship between archaeology and religion, and that subsequently
the archaeology of religion will be adequately theorised; it will
not be. For in stating this it should be accordingly noted that
archaeological approaches to religion have been remarkably naïve
and it has frequently been thought of as a relatively simple area
of investigation. It is not, as it is comprised of the residue associated
almost wholly with people's beliefs, both individual and collective,
and thus it is in fact remarkably complex.

However, this is not reflected in existing literature. Previous
studies of archaeology and religion have tended to be very general
(Renfrew 1994a; Fagan 1998), concerned with a single religion –
Christianity or Islam for example (Frend 1996; Insoll 1999a),
elements thereof (Rodwell 1989), world religions alone (Insoll
2001a) – or have appeared as conference proceedings with their
usual eclectic focus (see, for example, Insoll 1999b, 2004;
Garwood *et al.* 1991; Carmichael *et al.* 1994; Goldsmith *et al.*
1992). Otherwise, 'ritual', the archaeologists' favourite catch-all

category for 'odd' or otherwise not understood behaviour, has been focused on, as will be described.

The neglect of religion by archaeologists can be seen in many of the major textbooks. In Bogucki's (1999) *The Origins of Human Society* for instance, written from a self-stated 'Republican Party view of human prehistory' (p. 26), thus invoking 'self-interest' as the mediating rationale behind prehistory, 'religion' is subsumed within 'ideology' in the index whilst 'ritual' gets its own category. In contrast, social organisation, inequality, elites, and systems of authority are all well served, but religion is reduced to an apparently little-mattering element of ideology best served by archaeologists within a ritual domain. Similarly, Robert Wenke's (1990) *Patterns in Prehistory*, though acknowledging that we should consider 'the higher level of the social, economic, and political relationships of peoples and social entities' (p. 311), aside from a brief consideration of the implications of Darwinism for religion, does not really engage with religion, ideas, or even ideologies as factors shaping the past. Again technology, environment, demography and economy are given precedence.

The two examples just chosen are American, but a similar absence of religion can be detected within textbooks on the other side of the Atlantic. Greene's (2002) *Archaeology: An Introduction* again lacks 'ritual' or 'religion' within the index, an obvious starting point. In terms of theorising religion, the general lacuna evident in archaeology is again reflected. Hence within the discussion of archaeological theory, 'making sense of the past', there is a consideration under interpretive archaeology of agency, ethnicity and gender as crucial variables of identity, but religion is absent. This is not to deny that relevant material is not included – some is. Greene (2002: 255), for example, provides a useful summary of discussion surrounding interpretation of neolithic henge monuments framed within a constructivist outlook, and rightly poses the question about archaeologists employing a range of 'philosophical, anthropological and sociological approaches to explore 'otherness', and although we might not want to create neolithic 'religions' (see pp. 53–9), hence perhaps the caution in using the label, an overall recognition that religion is also a key variable in the construction of identity/identities is required archaeologically.

A similar point can be made with regard to the second example chosen, Clive Gamble's (2001) *Archaeology. The Basics*. This is prefaced with the point that the book is not a textbook, and 'makes no attempt at comprehensive coverage' (p. xiii); but surely, it could be suggested, religion is a basic element which should be considered by archaeologists. For again Gamble provides an excellent introduction to all aspects of interpreting the past, but the absence of religion does seem like a basic omission within, for example, the useful consideration provided of archaeology and identity. Identity is well theorised and the point that it should be conceptualised 'as a set of overlapping fields' (2001: 206) can be agreed with, though it can equally be suggested that one of these fields could be religion (or alternatively as is argued later, it can be the overarching framework into which the other identity variables can be fixed), alongside ethnicity, nationalism, or gender.

Yet not all examples of archaeology textbooks neglect religion, and again positive examples can be chosen from both sides of the Atlantic. D.H. Thomas's *Archaeology* (1998), includes religion within the archaeology of the human mind (i.e. under the aegis of cognitive approaches). Although the essential premise of cognitive processualism can be critiqued (see p. 92), and the emphasis upon the analysis of 'past ritual behaviour' as 'archaeology's major contribution to the study of religion' not necessarily concurred with (see p. 12), nor his definition of religion likewise agreed with, at least religion is recognised. Similarly, Renfrew and Bahn's *Archaeology. Theories, Methods, and Practice* (2000) also fully recognises religion as approachable within the archaeological record. This is again framed within a cognitive archaeological perspective, in this instance derived primarily from Renfrew's approach to the archaeology of cult and religion, which can likewise be critiqued (see p. 96), but once more religion is present.

At this juncture it should be noted that the criticisms just made are not personally aimed at Gamble, or indeed at Wenke, Bogucki or Greene, and perhaps their volumes are easy targets for criticism, being mainstream textbooks or introductory texts not able to consider all subject areas. However, the point can be extended away from individuals to the archaeological community as a whole for archaeology and religion, both in its theoretical and methodological consideration, has been almost completely neglected to date. Hence this volume aims to begin to rectify this previous neglect, and it is conceived of as serving as an introductory statement/opening dialogue on the theory and methodology of the archaeology of religions.

The focus is thus not upon providing a gazetteer of religious sites, or upon typology, or historical process (though obviously the relevant historical background is referred to where necessary). Equally, no claim is made that everything is included; much of relevance has had to be consciously omitted, partly for reasons of brevity. Rather, the emphasis will be upon considering how the archaeology of religion has been approached both theoretically and practically, through considering previous research and a variety of minor, and three major case studies, the latter focusing upon aspects of archaeology and religion in West Africa.

Neither does this volume provide a defence of religion or serve the purpose of promoting religion; it is not generated by theology, defined by Byrne (1988: 3) as 'an attempt to express or articulate a given religious faith'. But equally, contra sceptical viewpoints, it is undeniable that religion, even if only defined as the residue of the opium of the masses (not the view taken here), indisputably constitutes a major area of archaeological evidence – quite how much is discussed below. Furthermore, this volume deliberately does not seek to define in hard facts what religion is, for it is illusory to pretend that such definitive facts can be simply proffered. Rather, to adapt a point made by Needham (1972: 223) in reference to paraphrasing Einstein on the laws of mathematics, 'so far as our categories refer to reality, they are not certain; and so far as they are certain, they do not refer to reality'. This is relevant for our purposes for, equally, statements which infer too much certainty with regard to interpreting the archaeology of religion are on the whole misleading and should be treated with suspicion, as will be described.

What then is this volume concerned with? It explores what are frequently defined as indigenous or traditional, prehistoric and world religions (for definitions, see pp. 8–9) – but predominantly with the former two as world religions; their material and approaches to their study have been extensively covered elsewhere (see, for example, Insoll 1999b, 2001a). This volume is both about what archaeology can tell us about religion, the definitional and theoretical problems inherent in approaching religion through archaeology, and also about the 'doing' of the archaeology of religion. It is both about the underpinning theory and the history of the archaeology of religion, and, through the case studies considered, the application of ideas to the archaeological study of religion. Finally, future research directions – again both methodological and theoretical – will be indicated with reference once again to Dafra, the Burkinabe shrine described in the Prologue.

## Definitions

The relevance of the archaeological study of religion within our discipline is profound, for a 'spiritual' dimension would seem to have been important to humankind since at least the upper palaeolithic (but see p. 32). Yet 'spiritual' and 'spirituality' are unspecific terms, of little use in defining what we seek to explore, invoking notions of belief, or perhaps generating images of faith healers, rather than the profound depths of religion. 'Spirituality' might be a component of religion, but remains as such, and its use by archaeologists is frequently a reflection of misunderstanding and the lack of debate as concerns definitions relating to religion. Similarly 'cult' is also a weak term, having connotations of something marginal, 'freakish', and occasional (i.e. not quite religious practice), but it is a term which has been used by some archaeologists (see, for example, Renfrew 1985; Carver 1993). Equally we are not concerned with magic – which in turn invokes superstition (see, for example, Merrifield 1987). Within this study there is a preference for the deliberate use of the term 'religion', and this needs defining, though in reality this is no easy task.

## *Religion*

The origins of the term 'religion' can, according to Bowie (2000: 22), be derived from the Latin translation of the Bible from Hebrew and Greek and attributed to Saint Jerome in *c.* the late fourth century CE, whilst Saliba (1976) argues that it is an explicitly Christian term which is only widely used from the Reformation. This in itself has important connotations as it can be suggested that the very term 'religion', which we use to describe practices, actions, rituals, beliefs and material culture, could in reality be of only limited utility, and in fact inappropriate to much of the material we as archaeologists consider. This is because it immediately sets up an explicit dichotomisation between what is 'religious' and what is not, when such simple divisions might not actually exist. It raises the question, which will be returned to again later, as to where does secular life end and religious life begin? Is religion as a concept really only the result of a desire to classify what is in effect an unclassifiable and indivisible facet of life for much of the world's population today and in the past? One could, if one was so inclined, perhaps suggest that 'religion' has been created as a 'discursive formation' along the lines of those described by Foucault (1985). It has been tidied up and placed in its 'correct' place, and thus defined along with 'medicine' or 'law' or 'economics' (Insoll forthcoming a).

Nonetheless, this stated, we shall have to use the term 'religion' to describe the subject of investigation considered in this book, for alternatives are hard to suggest. Yet if we consider 'religion' is it really that easy to define? It is not, and what religion is, and what it is composed of, has been the subject of much debate. Existing definitions of religion cover a wide spectrum and range from simple definitions such as that provided by Edward Tylor that religion is composed of 'the belief in spiritual beings' (1958: 8, cited in Bowie 2000: 15), or Émile Durkheim's sociological view that religion 'is a set of beliefs and practices by which society represents itself to itself' (Cladis 2001: xx), through to much more complex ones. An example of the latter is provided by Byrne (1988: 7): 'a religion is an institution with a complex of theoretical, practical, sociological and experiential dimensions, which is distinguished by characteristic objects (gods or sacred things), goals (salvation or ultimate good) and functions (giving an overall meaning to life or providing the identity or cohesion of a social group)'. Whilst a mid-point between the two is provided by Durrans's (2000: 59) definition that religion is 'a system of collective, public actions which conform to rules ("ritual") and usually express "beliefs" in the sense of a mixture of ideas and predispositions'.

We can also define further elements frequently associated with religion, thought of either as subsumed within religion or operating in parallel with it, as in Paden's (1994: 10) definition that religion is 'a system of language and practice that organises the world in terms of what is deemed "sacred"'. The notion of the 'sacred' being itself defined by Hinnells (1995: 437) as derived from the Latin *sacer* meaning 'consecrated to a divinity', and couched in more human terms by Geertz (1968: 98) with regard to religious beliefs as 'a light cast upon human life from somewhere outside it'. Whereas in contrast 'holy', another term frequently used in conjunction with religion, was derived from languages of North European origin and has its root in terms standing for 'health' or 'wholeness' (Hinnells 1995).

So what then is religion? In many respects it is indefinable, being concerned with thoughts, beliefs, actions and material, and how these are weighted will vary; but, in general terms, the simpler the definition the better. The important point to make is that regardless of all the complexities of definition which have been attempted – we have to recognise that religion also includes the intangible, the irrational, and the indefinable. Religion does not only function within a logical framework, it is also 'a system constructed by a long tradition of thought about fundamental human problems – life, love, good, evil, death' (Meslin 1985: 39); in other words, the essential concerns of the human condition. Clifford Geertz (1968: 95), though essentially anti-definition, also provides a thoughtful overview of what religion is in that it has a 'formative impact upon common sense, the way in which, by questioning the unquestionable, it shapes our apprehension of the quotidian world of "what there is"'.

## *Classifying religion*

As religion has been the subject of debate so have its supposed types. These are usually divided into two main classificatory groups: world religions (Christianity, Judaism, Islam, Hinduism, Buddhism, etc.) and traditional/primal religions (African religions, Australian Aboriginal religions, etc.). The features of world religions are defined by Bowie (2000: 26) as:

1  Based on written scriptures.
2  Has a notion of salvation, often from outside.
3  Universal, or potentially universal.
4  Can subsume or supplant primal religions.
5  Often forms a separate sphere of activity.

Whereas those of traditional/primal religions are defined by Bowie (ibid.) as:

1  Oral, or if literate, lacks written/formal scriptures and creeds.
2  'This worldly'.
3  Confined to single language or ethnic group.
4  Form basis from which world religions have developed.
5  Religious and social life are inseparable.

Although we need to separate our religious forms, and the terms 'world' and 'traditional' are used here, again for a lack of viable alternatives (and a lack of space to consider possible alternatives), rigid categories of identification criteria such as those just given are dubious (see Shaw 1990 for critique). Some apply, others do not, and Bowie's point that such 'categorizations are not without utility, or they would not have survived so long' (2000: 26) can also be disagreed with. Though it should also be noted that Bowie points out their limitations in indicating that they are

8

'at best intellectual constructs rather than descriptions of reality' (ibid.).

People think they need classificatory categories (see p. 139 below, and Foucault [1970] 2002, 1977), but it could also be argued that people have also been lazy, hence such classificatory categories have survived for so long, and if we examine these criteria for religious categorisation in greater detail weaknesses soon emerge. For example, point 5 under the classification for primal religions – 'religious and social life are inseparable' – can equally apply to world religions as well, with Islam providing a case in point, it being frequently described as 'more than a religion but a way of life' (Insoll 1999a: 2). Point 3 in both schemes, positing universality versus ethno- or language-specific distinctions, is equally flawed. Aspects of African traditional religions, for instance, are found across ethnic or linguistic boundaries, raising the question upon which criteria are such distinctions raised?

In effect, what has occurred is that religious systems have become 'typologized' (Barnes 1997a: 21) thereby invoking notions of 'great' and 'little' traditions, the great traditions usually correlating with literate world religions such as Christianity or Islam, and the little traditions, 'fragmented, localized, and largely associated with illiteracy' (ibid.), posited as correlating with primal, small-scale, or traditional religions. Such typologies are neo-evolutionary in tone, as Rosalind Shaw (1990: 342) has noted: 'a higher value is either implicitly or overtly ascribed to "world religions" or "universal religions" than to "traditional religions" or "primal religions"'. Better is a point made by Byrne (1988: 12) that religions are really only defined by variability within 'and variability of the general phenomenon'. Here, archaeology can contribute much to indicating that religions often have blurred edges, they overlap and traditions interplay in syncretic forms, rather than slotting into neatly defined rigid typologies (see Chapter 4). The question can also be asked as to why if religion and its supposed forms therein are so complex, the term 'ritual' is used most frequently as a descriptive device by archaeologists.

## *Ritual*

But first definition needs to be considered again. Ritual is both action and mental activity combined, and can be both sacred and secular, but as Zeusse (1987: 405) notes, 'although it would seem to be a simple matter to define ritual, few terms in the study of religion have been explained and applied in more confusing ways'. Ritual might seem straightforward, especially in the way it has been interpreted by archaeologists, but in fact it is not (Bell 1992, 1997). As Brück (1999: 314) notes, archaeologists may 'feel they know what ritual is but, on closer inspection, the picture becomes rather less clear'. Bowie (2000: 154) usefully describes rituals as 'multi-faceted'. This is an important point, as they are not merely concerned with physical action; instead they have this element usually in combination with 'passive and active modes of communication (verbal and non-verbal), esoteric and exoteric knowledge, often in the context of heightened emotional states'. Thus here, ritual is described as having emotion, experience (knowledge), movement and communication combined.

The complexities of ritual can be acknowledged as involving more than just inexplicable material, the category often ascribed as 'ritual' by archaeologists. The 'material manoeuvres' (Durkheim 2001: 314), which archaeologists might and do frequently consider ritual to solely be the residue of, 'are merely the external envelope concealing mental operations' (ibid.). Peel back the surface of ritual and it can be seen to be embedded within, and inseparable from, all the other diverse facets which comprise religion.

Ritual has been usefully described by Jonathan Smith (1980: 114) as a 'focusing lens' for the sacred, one which need not only be concerned with the odd but also with 'routine action'. However, Smith's definition of ritual is explicitly concerned with the sacred aspect of ritual, with its possible panoply of distinctive places and times, special clothes and equipment, and altered manner of speech (ibid.). Here, ritual functions to protect against what Zeusse (1987: 415) terms 'the encroaching banality of ordinary life'. Yet it also has to be remembered that many other activities besides those which might overtly be called sacred or religious can also become ritualised. The sequence of retrieving tools, for instance, might not only be the workings of a functional *chaine operatoire* but the result of an established ritual conferring perceived success on the technical operation being pursued, and here context will be critical in beginning to assess underlying ritual intent.

Archaeological definitions of, and approaches to, ritual have been varied (see, for instance, Brück 1999). Ian Hodder (1982: 164), for example, indicates how 'archaeologists use the term ritual for the two closely connected reasons that what is observed is non-functional and is not understood'. Hodder (1992: 222–3) posits that there is also a correlation within archaeology between 'ritual' and 'odd', a situation described as inadequate for defining ritual. This is certainly a recurring problem within archaeological approaches to ritual; the unexplained or the otherwise unexplainable is defined as such. Ritual is frequently seen within archaeological discourse as linked with burials, politics, or ideology, but not religion. It is in many instances treated simplistically.

In reality ritual is not simple. What is required is a more complex understanding of what ritual is by archaeologists. Bell (1997), for example, defines various elements which can form part of ritual. These include:

- *Formalism*: The formality of activities.
- *Traditionalism*: 'The attempt to make a set of activities appear to be identical to or thoroughly consistent with older cultural precedents' (ibid.: 145).
- *Invariance*: 'A disciplined set of actions marked by precise repetition and physical control' (ibid.: 150).
- *Rule-governance*: Self-explanatory.

Yet to recognise the subtleties and complexities of ritual will require definition on a case-by-case basis: ritual can be both odd and routine, it can be undertaken within the prism of the 'focusing lens' or elsewhere; it is both the context *and* the act which are crucial in understanding ritual.

However, ritual should not be thought of as equating with religion in terms of parity. It is an element thereof, but often it is treated as the descriptor for religion itself in archaeological parlance. Lewis (1980: 10) has made the apt point, though not in the context of archaeology, that ritual is often used 'as an adjective of compromise'. Within the proceedings of the 'Sacred and Profane' conference for example (Garwood *et al.* 1991), one of the first conferences explicitly held on archaeology and religion and one which recognises that religion/ritual(s) can give meaning to life and 'are of focal importance for the interpretation of past societies in general, and specific archaeological contexts in detail' (ibid.: v), ritual in both role and definition is given prominence when some of the material thus defined/described would be better accommodated within a religious framework, thus invoking the whole rather than the part.

Even Brück (1999), in her engaging consideration of ritual theory and interpretation in European prehistory, though acknowledging the possibility of the pervasive nature of ritual, fails to place ritual within its wider religious framework. Ritual is an element of the wider whole, and its archaeological recovery should be a reflection of this rather than a means to an end in itself. 'A religious world is an inhabited place', as Paden (1994: 57) notes, not a dehumanised set of ritual actions as it is sometimes presented by archaeologists. No ritual stands by itself – it sits within 'thick' context. Even if we cannot necessarily retrieve this context, we should acknowledge its former existence. Concentrating upon ritual alone might give us 'beautiful structures', to adapt a point of Gerholm's (1988: 199–200), but it does not provide the embedded overview.

## *The archaeology of religion*

What then is the archaeology of religion? In the view of this author it can be conceived of as the superstructure into which all other aspects of life can be placed – it is not necessarily a stand-alone category. For it is now recognised as important that many elements of life can be structured by religion, and can be archaeologically recognisable as such, above and beyond the usually considered domains of sacred sites and burial (see, for example, Hubert 1994, Insoll 1999a). This is not in the sense of some form of idealistic religious 'totality' as might be generated by Mircea Eliade, for example, the mythical total religious immersion of all people in all time juxtaposed against the predominantly secular historical 'time that kills' (Horia 1969: 387–8), but rather, by way of contemporary analogy, how all aspects of Islamic material culture can be structured by religion (Insoll 1999a).

## The individual perspective

Yet making this statement does not mean that everyone everywhere believed in god(s) all the time. People obviously do not today, and similarly they did not in the past. An essentialist view of the individual, or indeed of the archaeology of religion, is not what is being created here. Equally, the variation in how belief is held is great, as Geertz (1968: 111–12) has succinctly argued – that for one person their 'religious commitments are the axis' of their whole existence, while for another, 'not necessarily less honestly believing' their 'faith is worn more lightly'. The recognition that all aspects of material culture can be structured by religious considerations is not an invocation of 'homo religiosus' – 'religious man'. This being a reference to the mythical creature fashioned by some historians of religion, and exemplified by Mircea Eliade (1969: ii), who has stated that 'to be – or rather, to become – a man means to be religious'. This is not so, but it is still worth remembering that even if one does not believe one can still live a seemingly religious life if, perhaps, the remainder of the group demands it – the resulting actions being accompanied by obvious material culture consequences.

In fact the individual choice manifest in believing (or seeming to believe) or not believing in god(s) is very much a feature of the recent past, and even today cannot uniformly be exercised. Within Saudi Arabia, for example, religious choice is limited to one option, Islam, and manifestations of active participation in this belief system are more or less a requirement to conform, and to be seen to be functioning within society. But such restrictions on individual agency do not necessarily influence archaeological interpretation as regards religion. This is because most relevant and, importantly, influential archaeological research, especially that relating to theoretical issues, is completed by people who can openly exercise their individuality. Thus the projections made back onto the past with regard to the extent of religiosity, for instance, might more fully be a reflection of the contemporary archaeologists' life ways, choices, and preoccupations rather than those which actually existed previously.

The importance of the individual and individual choice certainly varies, and as Johnson (1999: 83) notes, there 'is no excuse for taking the modern Western "cult of the individual" as self-evident, or true for all times and all places'. The 'consciousness of self' (La Fontaine 1985: 124) might be universal, but the 'social concept of the individual' (ibid.) is not. As the studies in Carrithers *et al.* (1985) indicate, the notion of the individual varies widely across the world today, and would have done so in the past as well. In India, for example, Dumont (1985: 95) describes how within Hinduism caste and the accompanying social control constrains the individual, but how world renunciation, as practised by holy men and ascetics, offers the opportunity to exercise individuality. Yet, as Dumont notes, the world renouncer cannot be described as exercising individuality analogous to the modern Western concept for he or she is 'outworldly', beyond the margins of society, whereas Western individuality is embedded in society – 'inworldly' individualism. Yet what we as archaeologists frequently do is project this peculiar notion of inworldly individualism onto the past when in reality it is suited to only a peculiar range of limited contexts.

Similarly, to assume that the notion of individual experience permeates all religion is not necessarily correct. Pascal Boyer (2001: 308), for instance, notes how 'most Eastern teachings are primarily about correct performance of various rituals and technical disciplines, rather than personal experiences as such' – and where an emphasis on 'subjective experience' is found, this could be due to influences from Western philosophy such as phenomenology (see pp. 38–9). The point just cited might be something of a generalisation concerning the religious practices of hundreds of millions of people, and we do not want to fall into the trap of defining some sort of simplistic division between 'the egocentrism of western thought and the sociocentrism' (Morris 1994: 193) of other cultures, but overall it is salient in making us cautious about projecting our own particular Western philosophy back onto the past, and past religions once again. Perhaps here, as we have necessarily touched upon philosophy, we can make the point in the language of this discipline that as archaeologists our hermeneutic as regards ontology is flawed epistemologically when it comes to considering religion.

The origins of the Western tradition of the individual are much debated (see Carrithers *et al.* 1985), and although the Reformation was undoubtedly of significance in this respect (see McGrath 1993), it is the Enlightenment which we shall briefly consider here. As Cassirer (1951: 135) notes, the Enlightenment was not 'an age basically irreligious and inimical to religion', but its legacy upon concepts of religion, including individual agency therein, and subsequently upon archaeological interpretations of religion, is profound. For beginning in the late seventeenth century, the growth of rationality, the subduing of superstitions, the further increase in the importance of the concept of the individual and the focus on 'identities and differences' (Foucault [1970] 2002: 157) as part of the obsession with classification all begin.

This was the result of the Enlightenment, described by Mautner (1997: 167) as 'characterised by belief in progress, expected to be achieved by a self-reliant use of reason, and by rejection of traditionalism, obscurantism and authoritarianism' (and see Cassirer 1951). These are all intellectual factors which have had a profound impact upon how religion and, importantly, interpretations of past religion have been conceptualised by Western academics. Yet much of the archaeology of religion was formed according to different intellectual frameworks and conceptions. Rationality, classification, the stressing of individuality, are not necessarily appropriate structuring criteria for assessing the archaeology of religions, especially if we want, hopefully, to strive for a fuller understanding of past meanings. This said, a 'pre-Enlightenment' mindset is an idealistic and unachievable condition, and it could be asked if a book such as this could have been written without such a philosophical 'revolution' having occurred; but at least we can recognise the possible impact of factors such as those just described upon our interpretations, and also the fact that alternatives exist, and that the archaeology of religions could be 'other' both in structure and meaning.

The rise in importance of the concept of the individual might be one factor influencing perception of religion; another is how the accompanying rise of empiricism led to a limiting of sources of evidence – not through removing them but through denigrating their value as non-rational. Young and Goulet (1994: 10), for instance, make the point that as a direct consequence of this 'western intellectuals began to dismiss dreams as against reason'. Interestingly, although we can hardly hope to recapture a 'pre-Enlightenment' state of mind as already noted, there has been a reversal within anthropology towards reintegrating dreams and 'extraordinary experiences' as sources of evidence to complement more traditional ones (see, for example, Jedrej and Shaw 1992; Young and Goulet 1994). This is not to say that their value is necessarily especially significant, just that our archaeological 'rationality', and the intellectual legacy which created it, can affect our understanding of religion and 'experience' in many ways. As Brück (1999: 317), one of the few archaeologists to have touched upon some of these issues, notes, 'scientific logic is prioritized as the only valid way of knowing the world'.

Similarly, Eliade, though much of his work can be criticised as ahistorical and idealistic (Saliba 1976), does make the relevant point that the development of 'profane culture' (1969: 68) is a relatively recent phenomenon. This notion can be adapted for our purposes here, meaning that the explicit dichotomisation inherent in the sacred and profane evident today is a recent creation, and that previously such a division was less bounded and the spheres of overlap between, for example, what made a dance entertainment as opposed to a religious occasion were more fuzzy. Both could co-exist, and even if the religious dimension was manifest only in the individual's head whilst they engaged in activity x or y, exist it could, and thus its residue would form part of the all-encompassing framework of the archaeology of religion, above and beyond the usually posited categories of 'religious' or 'ritual' material culture such as temples or burials that we are familiar with.

Yet equally it has to be recognised that not everyone entertains religious thoughts all the time. As Morris (1987: 179) notes: 'there is a pragmatic and material dimension to human life, and the "sacred" is never total'. This is an idea which Kemp (1995) has pursued through archaeological evidence from Ancient Egypt for example. Starting from a sceptical position and a self-stated intention of overturning the usual view of Egypt as exemplified by the writings of Herodotus – for instance, that the Ancient Egyptians were 'religious to excess, beyond any other nation in the world' (p. 26) – Kemp argues that overall, in such a complex society as manifest in the New Kingdom city of Tell el-Amarna, people took the middle ground in religious belief and practice. Namely, that for most of them 'life is likely to have been a basically secular experience in which religion had a place of utility' (ibid.: 50), but that this varied according to the individual and individual circumstances.

This is a perfectly realistic position based on the interpretation of the presence and absence of relevant archaeological material such as votive objects and shrines. But could this absence of religiosity, or rather its moderated character, equally be a peculiar reflection of the circumstances, as Kemp himself recognises (ibid.: 29), of the evidence from a city founded by the Pharoah Akhenaten who was himself a monotheist, allied with factors such as the extent of the excavations and the visibility of the offerings made, rather than an overall reflection of the religiosity of the Ancient Egyptians. Kemp recognises these limiting factors, and the necessary realisation is apparent that to extend the interpretation of the degree of religiosity evident from one site or period even, to that of a complete 'people' or cultural group over time, is foolhardy.

Claude Lévi-Strauss (1973) is less cautious in his comments made following a visit to the Indus civilisation sites of Mohenjo-Daro and Harappa, the Indus civilisation being in some respects a comparable state formation to Egypt, certainly in its mature phase dating from *c.* 2500–2000 BCE. Lévi-Strauss refers to the 'disconcerting spectacle' of the planned streets with their sewers and identical dwellings, and the 'flimsy trinkets and precious jewels . . . indicative of an art devoid of mystery and uninspired by any deep faith' (ibid.: 163). Here a gross generalisation is being made about the extent of religion based on archaeological evidence. But is it really so clear cut? It is not, and the important point is that a sort of evolutionary paradigm is in effect being resurrected. A paradigm whereby 'primitive' peoples are somehow seen as more religious, whereas those of more 'developed' state systems are seen as more similar to the perceived modern condition. In reality complexity is the key, and the only way to approach degrees of religiosity through archaeological evidence is to recognise this – variability as evident both individually and communally – but without binding rules as to what degree is evident according to which social system is in operation.

Thus the possibility exists that religious beliefs/thoughts can structure all activity, regardless of the social system being considered. We as archaeologists at least have to recognise that this possibility exists. The point has been made that the absence of religion in much archaeological interpretation is in all probability more a reflection of the archaeologists' viewpoint rather than past realities, allied with the fashions which archaeology as a discipline, like anything else, is influenced by. In this respect, plainly, for a long time religion was (and is) unfashionable in the parts of Western society from which many archaeologists derive. This can but affect archaeological interpretation, but is not unique to archaeology alone. With reference to anthropology, Evans-Pritchard (1965: 100) made the point that (in the early 1960s) 'religion has ceased to occupy men's minds in the way it did at the end of the last, and at the beginning of this, century' – a generalisation which an anthropologist is unlikely to make today.

## *The numinous*

However, having made this point, the archaeologist interested in religion also has to recognise that they cannot get in the heads of past peoples (but see pp. 92–7 for cognitive approaches). Perhaps this can be achieved partially through our approximations of the past; but equally we have to be aware of our limitations and, if anything, recognise, certainly within the religious dimension, the existence of the 'numinous'. This is a term derived from the Latin *'numen'*, or 'supernatural entity', and is best thought of as the irreducible essence of holiness which can be discussed but not defined (Sharpe 1986: 164).

The 'numinous' was a concept developed by Rudolf Otto (1950), and although the remainder of his work is of little use for our purposes, and indeed the very existence of the numinous has been criticised for a lack of evidence (Sharpe 1986: 165), or for it being built upon Jewish and Christian examples (Byrne 1988: 19), it does provide a starting point for a required conceptual framework; that the sacred element in religion, and thus the archaeology of religion, comprises more than the material, something often abstracted in archaeological studies, and a recognition which allows study to move beyond merely cataloguing religious buildings and artefacts and thinking that is the sum total of the archaeology of religion. Religion is as much composed of 'private worlds or imaginary universes' (Eliade 1969: iv) as it is of its more accessible material facets. The recognition of the numinous equates with the fact that, as Meslin (1985: 47) notes, 'we are exploring a human dimension that is quite constant yet often mysterious and extratemporal'. It is in true definition, metaphysical – in the meaning of lying beyond nature (Mautner 1997: 351); acknowledgeable but irreducible. We can pose questions about its existence, but again we return to the metaphysical conundrum as defined by Scruton (2002: 4) in regard to scientific inquiry: questions can be generated that we lack the ability to answer.

A further important point about the recognition of the numinous is that it also allows for individual agency. It seems to offer, as Sharpe (1986: 161) notes, 'a defence of individualism, spontaneity and immediate experience'. Although the privileging of individual perspective was critiqued below, recognition of the individual is also vital within the archaeology of religion, but equally a recognition not undertaken at the expense of the communal as well. As noted previously, both are crucial scales of analysis with neither one nor the other allowed to dictate all interpretation – a mix-and-match approach to suit context and circumstance being the most appropriate perspective to employ.

Within archaeology the concept of the numinous has been little acknowledged, explored or applied. Colin Renfrew (1994a: 48), one of the few archaeologists to have actually considered religion (see pp. 96–7), has criticised the fact that 'the existence of such an experience in the past seems to be an assumption which the student of early religion has to make'. Renfrew is correct, for in many ways the projection of the concept of the numinous into the past is an assumption, rendered such by its very philosophical foundations, its personal, irreducible, and irretrievable nature – but, it could be argued, to deny it even for the upper palaeolithic is to deny religion a key element of its composition. Furthermore, to deny it would be fundamentally to weaken the very foundations upon which Renfrew's cognitive processualism rests (see p. 92) by removing an element of the universal 'we' upon which many of its assumptions rely. This is the 'we' which links past and present and which underpins cognitive processual interpretative assumptions – for to deny the numinous element of religion is to deny an undeniable contemporary aspect of much of humanity's experience of the past, and in so doing weakening the universal humanist position linking past and present, which is a crucial element of cognitive processualism.

## Fideism – the position of faith

But does recognition of the numinous presume that the archaeology of religion should be approached from the perspective of faith? This is not a proposition accepted here, for it is also the case that a position of faith can be a limiting factor in the archaeological study of religion – in questioning established doctrines of world religions, for example (see pp. 60–4) – if approached from what equates to a believer's perspective. Conversely it could also be argued, again with regard to world religion, that it is possible that something might be lost through not being an adherent or believer in the religion being studied; one might not be able to see the complete whole if detached from it (see Insoll 1999a: 7–9).

This also introduces the concept of 'belief' – linked to the numinous and the irreducible and in itself a deceptively simple term. 'Belief' has been described by Needham (1972: 4) as seen as 'a word of as little ambiguity as "spear" or "cow"', when in reality, 'more than two hundred years of masterly philosophical application have provided no clear and substantial understanding of the notion of belief' (ibid.: 61). This complexity recognised, it is still correct to state that in general a faith or believer's perspective in approaching the archaeology of religion too often leads to a theological or 'proof' emphasis being established, and elsewhere in this context this author has argued that archaeologists studying religion 'might profit, though following neither the agenda of theologically driven religious fundamentalism, nor atheism or agnosticism' (Insoll 2001b: 9). Supposed objective rationality or believer's emotion? Neither is a useful framework from which to appreciate the archaeology of religion.

But equally it should not be denied that an experience of religion is unnecessary; it is, as Evans-Pritchard (1965: 121) has noted, for religion can be better understood 'by one in whose inner consciousness an experience of religion plays a part'. Yet in making this point, a cry for a phenomenological experience of universal religion is not being made (see p. 38), this being the idealistic and unachievable aim of some historians of religions. Instead, what is required is a recognition of the numinous, but also an awareness that there is more to religion (and its resultant archaeology) than it merely being the result of an 'illusion' (ibid.), or a delusion suffered by the participants involved.

21

## *The archaeology of religion*

The archaeology of religion is complex, and, put simply, the material implications of the archaeology of religion are profound and can encompass all dimensions of material culture. If religion cannot be seen as the structuring principle for the lives of past communities the question can be posed as to what proof is required? Perhaps 80 per cent of the world's population live life today where religion provides the overarching framework for other aspects of life, at least as outwardly manifest, yet our conceptions of past religiosity, or rather the lack thereof, are defined by the remaining 20 per cent (Figure 2). The more we look, the more we can see religion as a critical element in many areas of life above and beyond those usually considered – technology, diet, refuse patterning, housing. All can be influenced by religion; they are today, why not in the past? Religion can be of primary importance in structuring life into which secular concerns are fitted, the reverse of the often-posited framework.

This, however, is not framed from a perspective of religious idealism but is merely a reflection of the fact that we also need to reflect critically on the questions we ask of the past, as well as the possible answers themselves. If the question of the influence of religion on past communities is not considered then many of the other questions we frame will be incomplete, predicated as they are upon the unrepresentative experience of a minor part of the world's population. To adapt the words of Paul Ricoeur (1985: 13), we have to 'confront the modern interpreter's horizon'. The archaeology of religion is a reflection of this and, properly defined, thus encompasses much more than that usually considered, such as religious/ritual sites (shrines, temples, sacred sites, churches, synagogues, etc.) (Burl 1981; Hachlili 2001), or burial evidence (Parker Pearson 1999); it is the framework into which all other aspects of archaeology, of past life, can be placed. All categories of evidence can (but need not) be of significance in the archaeology of religion, and it is this notion, among others, which will be considered in some detail in the following chapters as potentially relevant across time.

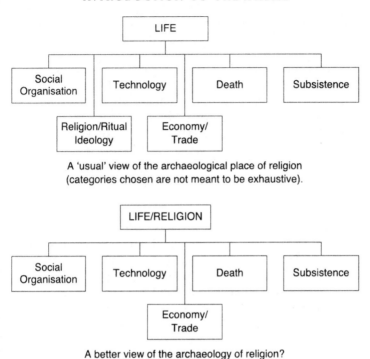

A 'usual' view of the archaeological place of religion
(categories chosen are not meant to be exhaustive).

A better view of the archaeology of religion?

*Figure 2* Two views of the 'place' of religion

## The origins of religion

Yet do we need to perhaps consider a temporal benchmark with
which to begin? When then can we speak of the origins of
religion? Is it the 'upper palaeolithic', or what would be referred
to in an African context as the Late Stone Age (LSA), or can we go
earlier into the middle palaeolithic, or Middle Stone Age? When
can the bottom end of our chronology be fixed? In truth this is not
at all certain, for the search for the origins of religion is a fruitless
one – a Holy Grail.

Nonetheless, debate persists over the origins of 'symbolic'
behaviour linked with what historians of religions call 'homo

symbolicus', defined by Ries (1994: 6) as being the result of imagination, meaning 'man [*sic*] grasps the invisible by means of the visible and can become the creator of culture and cultures' – the search for which returns us in many respects to the fixation with the origins of religion which dominated research from 1870 to the end of the nineteenth century (Sharpe 1986: xii). Hence we get evolutionary trajectories apparent in examples of archaeological research, as is evident in the contents pages to E.O. James's (1957) book *Prehistoric Religion* whereby the reader is led through 'the Cult of Skulls' in the palaeolithic, and subsequently onwards in time and accompanying religious manifestations.

This also again raises the pertinent issue of terminology. For with history of religions, 'homo symbolicus' seems, consciously or unconsciously, to be usually associated with ritual, whereas religion is differentiated and is linked with a new creation, 'homo religiosus', as already described (see p. 13). If we use Ries's (1994) work as an example (admittedly a glossy popularist volume but written by a noted historian of religions), we can chart an evolutionary framework from 'symbolicus' to 'religiosus' over a stated two-million-year time period linked to a (mis)interpretation of archaeological data. Australopithecines are discounted as disappearing 'without leaving traces of culture', whereas, 'the message of implements and traces of fire rites and funeral rites makes it clear that the passage from *Homo habilis* to *Homo erectus* and *Homo sapiens* entails a sacred experience' (Ries 1994: 146). It is related to what Cladis (2001: xvii) would describe as a 'delirious' interpretation hinged around 'the human imagination in confrontation with such natural phenomena as lightning, wind, stars, or fire' (ibid.). The upright posture associated with bipedalism is also seen as allowing an appreciation of landscape, its features, and distant horizons, these being, in turn, an impetus to, and crucial in, the developmental process of 'symbolization', contemplating the 'vault of heaven', and 'the psychic life of man and his perception of transcendency' (Ries 1994: 150).

Here archaeology is subsumed within a grand schema which seeks the origins of religion through 'symbolic' behaviour, and then in turn leading to the development of 'religious' behaviour. It is an example of the grand narrative, whereby archaeological evidence is a subservient source in a process of 'moving backwards through history' (ibid.). The context of the word 'history' is key as a methodological, and indeed, theoretical pointer within the history of religions, as opposed to the concept of 'prehistory' as used by archaeologists, and indicating how religion is seen, even though wholly inappropriate, as something that can be read like text, back to the beginnings of hominid origins. Similar criticisms can be made of Eliade's use of archaeology in the search for the origins of religion. The existence of a 'primordial age' (1969: 25) is posited and placed before the palaeolithic, an era described as being beyond investigation, thus denying an entry into 'what prelithic man thought during many hundreds of thousands of years' (ibid.). Thus here, obviously, a fictional era is created, and in other respects time itself is also being denied by Eliade; instead a mythical ahistorical time is created.

How then do archaeologists view the origins of religion today? First, it has to be stated that the term 'religion' is not really used to define such a search. Instead, where what is being sought is actively considered, it is framed within alternative terminology. Paul Mellars (1996) for example, avoids the use of 'ritual' or 'religion' and instead positions that element of his enquiry within, broadly, 'symbolism', with symbol defined as 'anything, be it object, sign, gesture or vocal expression which in some way refers to or represents something beyond itself' (ibid.: 369). This is fine; the scarce evidence from the middle palaeolithic which might attest to symbolic behaviour can hardly be used to construct 'religion'. However, again one could posit the suggestion that although 'religion' or 'ritual' might be wholly inappropriate, is not part of the potential definitional problem perhaps due to the fact that what is being described or sought is irreducible anyway? Thus we might get, rightly, recognition of developing 'consciousness' (Lewis-Williams 2002: 190), or 'cognitive fluidity' (Mithen 1998: 209), placed within the perspective of cognitive processualism; but to push the discussion on without the later material clues we might get, which at least allows partial consideration of religion, is to attempt to define the origins of the indefinable and the wall of the numinous is encountered.

But this said is it necessary to be entirely pessimistic? Although it has been stated that the search for the origins of religion are fruitless we can at least allow archaeological evidence to steer our understanding of when the behavioural and, by implication, mental complexity for religious belief might have begun to be in place. For, as it has hopefully been shown, religion is undeniably complex, and, divine inspiration aside, the necessary nurturing conditions of mental complexity and physical proficiency are essential for its success.

In this respect it is perhaps necessary, based upon recent research, to shift the discussion to Africa and the Middle Stone Age, rather than seek, as has often been the case, such conditions in European prehistoric contexts for example. For the cogent point has been made by McBrearty and Brooks (2000: 534) that the search for the supposed upper palaeolithic 'revolution' of sudden and seemingly simultaneous modern behaviour (of which 'religion' would conceivably be a part) throughout the Old World $c$. 40,000–50,000 years ago is flawed, in that such perceptions are a result of 'a profound Eurocentric bias in Old World archaeology that is partly a result of research history and partly a product of the European material itself'. Equally, the very attributes of modernity, the nurturing conditions referred to previously, have been recently critiqued as reflecting Eurocentric assumptions. Wadley (2001: 210), for example, has taken umbrage with the 'shopping list' approach to its recognition and the presumption of the full package developing at once – exactly what upper palaeolithic 'revolutions' imply. Instead she rightly argues that manifestations of modernity could include all or some evidence indicative of the development of art, personal ornamentation, style in lithics and the formal use of space.

To these could perhaps be added other categories, but it is certainly in Africa that the evidence does seem to conspire to indicate that the earliest indications of 'modern' behaviour are to be found, and equally that these are to be linked with the early modern forerunners of ourselves, *Homo sapiens sapiens*. Although this is an area of research subject to polarised opinions and heated debate, the DNA data suggests, in the words of Paul Mellars (1989: 350), that the higher degree of internal genetic variability evident, more than elsewhere in the world, means 'an initial emergence of genetically (and presumably anatomically) modern human populations within Southern Africa'.

The emergence of early modern humans is dated to approximately 150,000–100,000 years ago, with the subsequent 'Out of Africa II' migration taking place from $c$. 100,000–80,000 years ago (Stringer and Gamble 1993: 38). DNA evidence is not necessarily convincing on its own, but it appears to be supported by early modern human skeletal remains recovered from the same region. The important site of Klasies River Mouth in South Africa yielded such remains, mostly from a horizon dated to 90,000 years ago, but also from other contexts dated to between 110–120,000 years ago – that is, long before anywhere else in the world. These, according to Deacon and Deacon (1999: 104–5), are not from conventional burials but show evidence of charring, 'impact fractures and cut marks', possibly consistent with cannibalism, 'inspired by ritual rather than hunger' (ibid.: 105).

Hence here we seemingly also have an indication of the type of behaviour we are interested in as well. We can also look at other facets of the evidence. The existence of the Howiesons Poort-backed blade industry at Klasies River Mouth, essentially displaying aspects of what would usually be defined as an LSA or upper palaeolithic technology in MSA contexts dated to between 80,000 and 60,000 years ago (see Wadley 2001: 203). Or an engraved fragment of mammal bone which was recovered along with two pieces of ochre 'deliberately engraved with abstract patterns interpreted as symbolic, meaningful representations' from Blombos Cave, another Middle Stone Age site also in South Africa (D'Errico et al. 2001: 309). These were found in contexts dated to $c$. 70,000 years ago, and other evidence concurring with Wadley's (2001) criteria for modernity recorded at this site included a stone-working activity area, circular hearths, and a worked-bone tool industry (D'Errico et al. 2001). To this could be added the African tradition of body ornamentation, described by McBrearty and

Brooks (2000: 521) as pre-dating 'that of Europe by tens of thousands of years'.

Therefore it seems fairly convincing that modern behaviour and anatomy was developed in Africa and from there spread out with early modern human populations to the rest of the world, in so doing replacing pre-existing populations, as evident (McBrearty and Brooks (2000) critique aside) in the rapid appearance of a host of new technologies, art forms, burial practices, ritual practices, alliance strategies, types of spatial use, etc. Similar evidence from 'our' closest 'competitors' is unconvincing in this respect. For example Neanderthal burial, though undoubtedly occurring, lacked the same degree of formalisation evident in burials associated with early modern human populations. This is a subject which has been considered in detail by a variety of scholars much better qualified to discuss this issue than this author, and from a variety of positions, both for and against (see, for example, Chase and Dibble 1987; Gargett 1989; Stringer and Gamble 1993; Parker Pearson 1999). But a moderate position, as adopted by Mellars (1989: 362), would seem to have to be agreed with; that is, that essentially, deliberate Neanderthal burial of the dead such as that evident at the sites of La Ferrassie, Le Moustier or La Chappelle-aux-Saints in France is 'difficult to contradict', but the claims for burial of grave goods such as those proposed for a ring of ibex horns found at Teshik Task in Uzbekistan, or a ring of stones around a Neanderthal skull at Monte Circeo, 'are open to some doubt' (ibid., and see Mellars 1996: 379).

Evidence such as that from Shanidar Cave in Iraq has been dismantled upon closer examination. Where instead of it indicating careful burial of a crippled Neanderthal adult male, seemingly with a bunch of fresh flowers laid in the grave (Solecki 1971), it might be that the burial niche was a natural one in which the injured man sheltered (Gargett 1989: 176). Even if the grave pit was intentionally dug, the pollen from the flowers, such as grape hyacinth and St Barnaby's thistle, could have been introduced by the wind (ibid.), or in the form of flower heads by a small rodent such as the Persian jird (Sommers 1999). Thus, as Sommers (ibid.: 128) notes, rather than the flowers indicating the universality of humankind, a love of beauty, and that Neanderthals had 'the full range of human feelings and experience' as proposed by Solecki (1971), they are the result of something much more prosaic.

Or is it in fact the intentional burial of a shaman? This has been suggested by Bean and Vane (1992: 9). An explanation proposed also by Pearson (2002: 65–6), who further talks about the 'medicinal properties' of the plants found at Shanidar. This is a critical interpretation, as the scholars just cited also refer to shamanism being an ancestral religion. 'Shamanism is arguably the oldest of human spiritual endeavours, born at the dawn of our species' awareness', as Pearson (ibid.: 162) states; whereas Hedges (1992: 88) describes shamanism as 'the basic religion of mankind'. Hence here, we seemingly have the 'original' religion – or do we? No, for it is probably too simplistic, attractive as it might be, to posit shamanism as the ancestral religion; the definitional problems surrounding the very category of 'shamanism' appear to render it unworkable as a cross-cultural and temporal religious label (see Chapter 4). Equally, it is unsophisticated to suggest there was one universal form of primal religion, as erroneous as to suggest 'animism' or 'totemism' might likewise be the ancestral religious form. It removes complexity, a precondition of religion now, in *all* its variants, and, it is suggested, similarly for the past.

More specifically, the taphonomic considerations surrounding the Shanidar Neanderthal burial described here cast doubt on its intentionality and certainly on its 'shamanic' character. Similar question marks have been raised over other indicators of Neanderthal behavioural complexity being on a par with that of early modern humans; art, forward planning, the mental templates required to produce stone and other technologies (Mellars 1996: 389), all can and have been questioned. Instead the 'cultural explosion' does seem to be most convincingly associated with our early modern ancestors. In this respect, a key difference which could have existed between early modern humans and others such as the Neanderthals might have been in consciousness. This is something which has been examined by Mithen (1998: 172), who has argued that the development of 'cognitive fluidity'

29

was crucial in the creation of 'the modern mind'. This, according to his thesis, involved the coming together of the four domains, or 'chapels' as he describes them, of technical, natural history, social and linguistic intelligence.

As this pertains to religion, it is suggested that it took place in two stages with totemism and anthropomorphic thought developing *c.* 100,000 years ago as a result of the integration of social and natural history intelligence. Then, *c.* 60,000–30,000 years ago, the addition of technical knowledge to this cognitive cocktail gave rise to animism, leading overall to Mithen's confident assertion that 'religious ideologies as complex as those of modern hunter-gatherers came into existence at the time of the Middle/ Upper Palaeolithic transition and have remained with us ever since' (1998: 202). Mithen further argues that early modern humans, perhaps similar to the populations of the MSA referred to previously, drifted in and out of cognitive fluidity, but that a 'partial cognitive fluidity was to prove absolutely critical in giving Early Modern Humans the competitive edge as they spread from Africa and the Near East throughout the world between 100,000 and 30,000 years ago' (ibid.: 209).

The problems with cognitive processualism, the theoretical framework in which Mithen's model sits, are described in Chapter 3, and the type of universalising perspective enjoyed is not that supported here (i.e. a defining 'hey-presto' moment of religious complexity subsequent to a number of evolutionary stages), but nonetheless it is an interesting argument, parts of which might help in explaining the evident differences between the archaeology of early modern humans, as described, and that of other populations.

Moreover, a key differential element might have been in linguistic competence. The proficiency of Neanderthals linguistically has been much debated, centring around, for instance, their potential physical maladaptation to language, possibly manifest in a higher-sitting larynx than that found in modern humans, though according to Johanson and Edgar (2001: 106) this can be disputed, and they argue that Neanderthals had an 'essentially modern morphology'. Yet once again Mellars (1996: 389) perhaps provides one of the most useful reviews of this issue through integrating a variety of evidence in considering Neanderthal language capability, and in so doing comes to the conclusion that proficient language existence amongst the Neanderthals can be disputed on three counts:

- The lack of anatomical ability (if such a lack existed) is an indication of 'the limited *need* for this capacity among Neanderthals'.
- The lack of convincing evidence for 'symbolism' is 'consistent with the lack of highly developed language in Neanderthal communities'.
- The templates evident in upper palaeolithic tool forms are less sharply defined for the middle palaeolithic and 'would fall naturally into place if the mental and associated *linguistic* categorization of different tool forms in the Middle Palaeolithic was much less tightly structured than in the Upper Palaeolithic'.

Now for our purposes here, language is crucial in the formalisation or at least continuation of ritual and religion. Manifestations of such might have existed in a Neanderthals' head but, even with the best efforts of neurophenomenologists (see pp. 40–1) or cognitive processualists, this will remain elusive to archaeologists. Furthermore, locking religion in the head (assuming this can be done without the ability for proficient external language existing, which hardly augurs well for complex abstract thought) would mean that it might function perfectly adequately at the level of the individual but its translation into group or wider contexts would be far from successful. Moreover, if Neanderthal consciousness was primarily domain-specific, and language conceivably limited, the elaboration of myth and the repetition of ritual would have been rendered very difficult, for it can be suggested that grunts, prods, and pointing are not the ideal means for perpetuating myth and ritual.

However, it might be salient at this juncture to admit that a far from exhaustive review of the relevant evidence has been achieved, and claims made in the defence as to the overall brevity of the study provided, but instead it is pertinent to note that the provision of such a review is unnecessary. Rather, the few selected examples have been chosen to illustrate that it is possible to begin to isolate where the required complexity for the development of religion was first apparent, and equally who it appears to have been associated with – us, at least in our early modern form. Yet once again the shortcomings of 'religion' as a descriptive term are all too apparent, for its use within this context suggests that modern parallels are being projected back into the African MSA, or onto the interface of the middle and upper palaeolithic. This is emphatically not the case. Furthermore, it is also necessary to take a step back from the picture just constructed in adding that we might be able to say that the criteria indicating modernity are beginning to be apparent, and that from this we might be able to begin to infer that the mental complexity required for religion was forming, but we can never be certain that:

- The assumption of similarity from *Homo sapiens sapiens* today back 70,000–90,000 years to early modern forms is valid (and similarly for other time frames as well).
- That the types of material inferred as indicative of non-functional, ritual, symbolic, religious, odd, or whatever behaviour was necessarily generated within such a frame of reference.

This perhaps is the pessimistic position, but it is essential to state it. The problems with analogy even within much more recent contexts are profound (and are discussed in Chapter 4), and rely, within these greater depths of time, on more than a fair share of presumption. Hence the archaeology of religion has no defined benchmark with which we can state that study can begin, and assertions to the contrary that claim to have identified the original 'shaman', 'ritual', 'religion', 'animist', 'totemic emblem' 'anthropomorphic manifestation' or the like, should be treated with suspicion.

# 2

# HISTORY OF RESEARCH

## Disciplinary frameworks

Recent research relevant to the origins of what might be termed 'symbolic behaviour' has just been described. Within this field, it could be suggested, most scholars involved would baulk at the use of the term 'religion' as applied to these early contexts – rightly, in most instances, as was noted. But definitional applications aside, overall the history of research into the archaeology of religion is a somewhat patchy one. The archaeology of religion has tended to be considered within the type of frameworks already defined, piecemeal, as part of something else, a single aspect perhaps rather than as a complete entity – a fact best indicated by the sometimes obsessional focus upon the archaeology of death and burial evident (see pp. 67–71), as opposed to considering the possible wider perspective, even though the evidence might permit this. The history of archaeological approaches to religion will be charted later, but prior to this we need to consider what other major disciplines there are involved in the study of religion.

This is necessary because archaeology does not, or should not, function in isolation, but cognate disciplines have tended to be ignored as a source of theory and method for the study of religion by archaeologists. This reticence is unusual as archaeologists could stand accused of grabbing large chunks of other disciplines without really understanding them, or at least without being able to apply them properly. A classic example is provided by philosophy, and this is a process outlined by Hodder (1999: 22) who describes how archaeologists became dependent on 'philosophy-led accounts which prescribed' what they should do, though in practice it was difficult to follow such schemes and thus they were prone to failure. More recently, though, Hodder (2001: 11) is more optimistic about the intellectual position of archaeology as regards its interdisciplinary relationships, and notes that archaeologists are 'contributing to wider debates not just borrowing'. Unfortunately, this statement is as yet untrue as regards the archaeological study of religion, which is not even at the level of borrowing, but remains at one of neglect.

## *Anthropology*

Within cognate disciplines such as anthropology, in contrast to archaeology, the study of religions is long and distinguished. The history and intellectual impact of this has been well charted elsewhere (Evans-Pritchard 1965; Saliba 1976; Morris 1987; Bowie 2000), and will not be repeated here. However, this said, it is worth while to note (Insoll 2001b: 4) that over the course of some 150 years of debate this does not mean that anthropologists have worked out the perfect theoretical and methodological approaches to religion; they have not. As Morris (1987: 2) points out, anthropological studies 'largely focus on the religion of tribal cultures and seem to place an undue emphasis on its more exotic aspects'. So-called tribal religions are thus split up into phenomena – myth, magic, witchcraft, etc. – whereas world religions are treated within a different theoretical framework as discrete entities such as 'Hinduism' or 'Buddhism'.

However, anthropological studies of religion, regardless of their sometimes arbitrary thematic division, do indicate the potential complexities inherent in the study of religion through archaeology. Perspectives within the anthropological study of religion have shifted since the 1960s, as described by Eriksen (1995: 198), as part of an overall general shift in anthropological thinking 'from an interest in functions, structure and social integration ... to a concern with the interpretation of meanings, symbols and social process'. Much of the research being generated is of great relevance for archaeologists exploring religion: Bowie's (1998) evaluation of feminist perspectives within anthropological studies of religion for example. In its nuanced deconstruction of the concept of the 'generic woman' and the 'generic man', thereby questioning the generation of supposed universalist paradigms, and, importantly, emphasising that the notion of 'monodiscursive' analyses based upon 'a rather static notion of the relationship between discourse and social action' (ibid.: 54), it is useful in indicating that this can be a simplistic approach to understanding religion.

Equally relevant is the notion of the individual and the person, and the frequent inappropriacy of Western-derived models for projecting onto contemporary cultures and groups, let alone back onto the past which we as archaeologists do; this has been eloquently considered by anthropologists (see Morris 1994, for example). These are critical concepts within the archaeological study of religion in defining the units of analysis required, as described, but still largely await the desired nuanced treatment from within our discipline, certainly with regard to religion. Overall, the possible complexities which exist are well-signalled in a point made by Demarest (1987: 372) who notes that, 'even in contemporary circumstances with living informants and known histories, the analysis of religion presents formidable obstacles to the scholar'. These obstacles, with the living informants removed, become even more difficult when confronted from an archaeological perspective.

## History of religions

Another discipline which has already been mentioned and which should be further briefly considered is the history of religions, or comparative religions, which encompasses various fields of study and also makes use of archaeological data, and could prove helpful for the archaeological study of religion as sources of both ideas and material. A further term sometimes applied to history of religions is *Religionswiffenschaft*, which is described by Hinnells

(1995: 416) as the academic study of religion apart from theology, and was introduced by Friedrich Max Müller (1823–1900). *Religionswiffenschaft* in German covers both science and humanities, a meaning which is largely lost in translation (Hinnells 1995), and which for our purposes serves to indicate the multidisciplinary nature of history of religions. This is because it is composed of a number of different sub-disciplines: history of religion (singular), psychology of religion, philosophy of religion, sociology of religion and phenomenology of religion, for example.

If we search deeper within these component parts of the history of religions we can begin to assess their potential for approaching the archaeology of religions. The psychology of religion, defined by Hinnells (ibid.) as the application of 'the theories and methods of psychology to the study of religious phenomena', would appear to be of little relevance. The same point about a lack of general relevance could also be extended to the philosophy of religion. Similarly, the sociology of religion, concerned as it is with the 'notion of rationalisation' (Morris 1987: 69), as exemplified in the work of scholars such as Durkheim (2001) and Weber (1963) with their emphasis upon empirical questions as to the social implications of 'what kinds of people hold what kinds of beliefs under what kinds of conditions' (Hinnells 1995: 486), does not appear to offer much of a way forward either. This is because although the realisation that religion has a socially integrative role as well is useful, as Saliba (1976: 159) notes: 'religion is never a perfect idealization of social and cultural reality'. The conventional history of religion, more a collection of facts and collation of dates and events than anything else, the whole usually lacking interpretation, is also inappropriate. Thus in answer to the initial query posed as to their potential for approaching the archaeology of religion the answer is primarily negative. This leaves the phenomenology of religion which is considered in greater detail on pp. 38–41.

This in turn raises the second question as to whether the archaeology of religions could be placed under this disciplinary framework as well. These are ideas which have been discussed elsewhere (Insoll 2001b: 5–7), and the conclusion which can be drawn is again negative. Historians of religion sought the essence of religion with an emphasis upon normative hermeneutics, 'revealing the essential aspects of the human condition' (Ries 1994: 6), and exemplified by the work of Mircea Eliade which has already been introduced, a scholar who placed an accent on religion, not history, and bemoaned particularism (Saliba 1976: 28). This differs from the historian of religion (singular) who 'examines the cults and beliefs within a particular religious tradition, [whereas] the phenomenologist makes a systematic analysis of the phenomena itself' (ibid.: 30), thus forming what would be termed within hermeneutics or the science of interpretation as 'descriptive hermeneutics' (Ries 1994: 6). Archaeology might form 'part of a battery of techniques applied to understanding such complex phenomena' as religions (Insoll 2001b: 6), but it should not, and need not, be subsumed within such an idealistic supra-discipline.

The misinterpretation of archaeological evidence by historians of religion has also already been described, and this can, in part, be ascribed to a naïve conception of what archaeology is: as a historical discipline, but not so much one concerned with events; as a literal source of evidence, rather than the more ambiguous creature it really is. Archaeology is utilised within the history of religions, which is fine; interdisciplinarity or multidisciplinarity is the only way to approach the study of religions, but instead of it just being drawn upon as a source of evidence an attempt is made to create the 'total hermeneutics' (Eliade 1969: 58), a new supra-discipline, and the history of religions is formed. Although Eliade (1978a: 43) might describe the history of religions as 'an impossible discipline' he attempts to create this supra-discipline, which fails in the demands it puts on the scholar, as is soon exposed when its constituent elements, such as the archaeological evidence drawn upon, are evaluated by archaeologists. True multidisciplinary scholarship is beyond the abilities of most, regardless of the point made by one historian of religions that 'to apply a single hermeneutic to religious realities necessarily defigures them in its reductionism' (Meslin 1985: 49).

Instead archaeological evidence could be used by historians of religions and within the study of comparative religions in an attempt to break down some of the rigid categorisation of religions and religious phenomena sometimes evident. An example of this is provided by Paden's (1994: 55) statement that 'if life is governed by cattle herding, the religious system will naturally reflect this'. This of course is not necessarily so, and archaeological evidence could indicate something of the diversity and alternative possibilities which could exist. This would appear to be something Paden himself would also be amenable to, as indicated by his plausible comment that, 'religions are not just static systems fixed once and for all, but continually interact with changes and reshape themselves accordingly' (ibid.).

But equally, as archaeology properly defined and understood might be of use within the study of comparative religions, or the history of religions, it also has to be recognised that archaeologists might learn from these disciplines as well. This is because it also has to be realised that the study of religion is, unsurprisingly, their primary business, and from aspects of the research completed within the history of religions or comparative religions archaeologists could derive some benefit – regarding the definition of ritual for instance (see p. 10), ritual having been treated in a much more nuanced manner by historians of religion (and anthropologists) than by archaeologists.

## *Phenomenology of religions*

Phenomenology was also a key theoretical and methodological tool used by historians of religion. Derived from the Greek 'phainomenon', 'that which shows itself' (Allen 1987: 273), the founder of the phenomenological movement, but not the first to use the term (see Moran 2000: 6–7), was Edmund Husserl who was the developer of the methodological practice of *epoché*, 'a Greek word meaning to "check" or "cease"' (Bowie 2000: 6). However, as Sharpe (1986: 224) notes, the impact of pure or transcendental phenomenology, as developed by Husserl, upon the phenomenology of religions was minimal apart from defining the 'general area of approach' and providing the 'principles of understanding', notably *epoché* and eidetic vision.

Both these 'principles of understanding' as the means of gaining an insight into religious experience, or 'overcoming the strait-jacket of encrusted traditions' (Moran 2000: 5), are essentially problematic. Eidetic vision, described as the means to acquire 'the essentials of a situation . . . an intuitive grasp of the essentials of a situation in its wholeness' (Sharpe 1986: 224), in its very definition can be seen to be idealistic and unachievable. Whilst *epoché*, used to internalise oneself within religion, 'the need to abstain from every kind of value judgement' (ibid.: 224), can and has been criticised for the very introspection it sets out to achieve, a criticism answered with the retort that it sets up an empathetic experience.

Whatever the debate upon the nature of the subjective or objective experience obtained, it is undeniable, as Hinnells (1995: 378) notes, that the question of introspection has 'totally blocked further development of the phenomenology of religion since 1970'. This was abandoned, primarily because of the difficulty involved in achieving empathy, i.e. the detached within, or what Bowie describes as 'methodological agnosticism' – something which can delude the scholar 'to assume that they are somehow neutral in their observations' (2000: 11). The idealism inherent in attempting to bracket or suspend the external world in favour of the 'experience itself' (Morris 1987: 176) was methodologically fatal. An internalised experience of each religion under study is an unachievable aim; subjectivity will creep into interpretations, but perhaps it is admirable in attempting to move away from what Sharpe (1986: 248) defines as 'a barren catalogue of what are taken to be religious 'facts' – though this said, the limitations of just what can be reconstructed using phenomenological methodology must be continually acknowledged.

This of course raises the issue of the universal suitability of phenomenology for archaeological data if the phenomenological notion of experience has proved such a stumbling block largely within a field, the phenomenology of religions, where the religions under study are living ones. How can we as archaeologists concerned primarily with the past and past 'experience' attempt to reconstruct this if the methodological hurdles are difficult enough for reconstructing extant experience? These are issues which will be returned to.

Phenomenology might have been abandoned as redundant by historians of religions, but more recently neurophenomenology has been developed (Peters 2000). Clack (in press) has recently examined the potential of this nascent discipline for the archaeological study of religion which he defines as giving 'primacy to researching the structure of the lived human experience' (ibid.: 2), with, in his view, success only possible through a neuro-phenomenological archaeology of religions having to 'explicitly acknowledge the subjectivity' of religious experience, and rightly, that a mix and match approach is necessary to 'navigate intermediary pathways between the philosophical milieu and cognitive neurobiology' (ibid.: 11, 17). But it is perhaps the case that because of these 'intermediary pathways' that subjectivity will always be elusive, precisely because of the neurophenomenological emphasis upon conflating biological approaches (the 'neuro') with philosophical ones (the 'phenomenology'). Seemingly, at face value, such a convergence might be possible, but in reality it leads to the union of the theoretical and methodological problems associated with phenomenology, as already described, with those surrounding biological approaches to religion as well.

In this latter respect, neurophenomenology could be criticised for being too bounded by sets of rules generated within a biological paradigm (see, for example, Peters 2000), and potentially also returning, in turn, to evolutionary frameworks as explanatory mechanisms for the development of complex phenomena such as religions. Within such biological approaches so called 'meta-theology' has been invoked, linked with 'neurotheology' which essentially reduces God(s), and religious experiences to 'issues of neural activity' (D'Aquili and Neuberg 1999: 199). A functional approach predominates in which, for instance, ritual is seen as 'integral to how the brain works' (Bell 1997: 32), and belief is often abstracted within attempts to define the universal correlates of the 'mentally reflexive self' (Crook 1995: 56).

A similar rationale could be said to structure psychological approaches to religion; as for example with McCauley and Lawson's (2002) study which draws upon an empirical and evidential base of developmental psychology, social psychology and neuro-psychology in attempting to assess the cognitive foundations of religion. Within such a framework a good attempt might be made at assessing the formation of ritual, but religion will remain elusive because belief cannot be scientifically tested in a neat way. By way of archaeological analogy it can be suggested that such studies look for the presumed methodological rigour of source analysis in approaching religion; the LA-ICP-MS (laser ablation inductively coupled plasma mass spectroscopy) for seek-ing the cognitive and psychological origins of religion – with religion as the block of material under analysis, variable in its composition perhaps, but ultimately analysable. Yet in the end, such biological and psychological explanations of culture, includ-ing those focusing upon religions, though seemingly persuasive, can be unpicked through their universality of emphasis, and in their attempt to reconstruct, rationalise, and systemise the irrational.

## A selected history of approaches

Allied with the earlier recognition that archaeologists have been unusually reticent in drawing upon other relevant disciplines in developing our theoretical and methodological approaches to religion we also have to recognise that we as archaeologists do not have a monopoly on the use of archaeological data. That pertaining to religion has been used by many others for various purposes, as has already been described, and the use of archaeo-logical evidence in such a way has a long history, stretching back to its utilisation within what could be termed 'evolutionary' approaches to religion. These shall initially be briefly considered before turning to the former treatment of religion by archaeolo-gists proper.

## *Antiquarian, evolutionary and early archaeological approaches*

Antiquarian investigations of archaeology and religion have been well documented. Stuart Piggott (1985: 53), for instance, in discussing the influences upon William Stukeley, the eighteenth-century English antiquary, refers to 'the literature of Druidism and the ancient Celtic religions from the Renaissance to the end of the seventeenth century'. Within these 'eight or ten' volumes is a book describing a potentially suspect find made in 1598 (but published in 1623) of a cinerary urn tentatively linked with Scythian, Indian, and Ethiopian burial customs, but ultimately said to be associated with a Druidic priest, Chyndonax. Druids figure prominently in these early antiquarian studies. Another influence upon Stukeley was the seventeenth-century English antiquary, John Aubrey, who interpreted the stone circles of Avebury and Stonehenge in Wiltshire as *'Templa Druidum'* (Piggott 1985: 51), 'temples of the Priests of the most eminent Order, viz. Druids' (Tylden-Wright 1991: 74). A theme continued and expanded upon by Stukeley so that, as Piggott (1985: 103) describes, the Druids became 'the enlightened priests of a religion by no means unlike that of the eighteenth-century Church of England' – to the extent that Druidical ceremonies at sites such as Avebury were thought to 'closely resemble the services in his own parish church at Stamford' (ibid.: 104). Overall, Stukeley presented a kind of Enlightenment conjectural history of religion in which monotheism was seen as a sign of a civilised society.

Another of the early uses of relevant archaeological evidence was within philosophical debate, as provided by the work of Hegel (1984, 1995) who uses it in his *Lectures on the Philosophy of Religion*. 'Proto' archaeological evidence is perhaps a better description, as archaeology was very much within its infancy as a discipline when these four series of lectures were presented between 1821 and 1831. Nonetheless, some Egyptological material is drawn upon, for example Belzoni's *Narrative of the Operations and Recent Discoveries within the Pyramids, Temples, Tombs and Excavations in*

42

*Egypt and Nubia*, as well as ethnographic sources and travel accounts for African and Eskimo (Inuit) religion (Hodgson 1995: 4–5, 8–9). However, the extent to which archaeology could be used as a source of evidence was obviously in part dictated by the availability of archaeological data, and overall it was not really used as a source of evidence until the second half of the nineteenth century.

Although Hegel employed an evolutionary perspective within his *Lectures*, a reflection on a progressive sequence of religions culminating in the ultimate, the 'consummate religion' of Christianity (Hegel 1998), it would be erroneous to classify his work along with, for example, James Frazer (see p. 44). The development of evolutionism post-dated Hegel, and equally it was not until the 1860s onwards that archaeology was 'laying bare the monuments of vanished civilisations', and, importantly for our purposes, 'overall was being spread the Darwinian canopy' (Sharpe 1986: 31).

The impact of Darwinian evolutionism was profound and archaeological evidence was employed within the construction of grand evolutionary religious sequences. Sharpe (ibid.: 52), for example, describes Lubbock's *The Origin of Civilisation and the Primitive Condition of Man*, published in 1870, as involving a six-rung evolutionary ladder comprising atheism, fetishism, totemism, shamanism, anthropomorphism and ethical monotheism. Interestingly, this concept of a ladder, though employed in the framework of discussing archaeological interpretation rather than religious evolution, and much later in date than the example just described, was to be used later by one of the first archaeologists to consider the feasibility of interpreting religion through archaeological evidence. This was Christopher Hawkes (1954: 161–2), whose 'ladder of inference' places technical processes on the bottom rung, followed by 'subsistence economics', social and political institutions, and finally 'religious institutions and spiritual life'. The latter is described as seeming superficially easy to examine, but in reality 'unaided inference from material remains to spiritual life is the hardest inference of all' (ibid.: 162) – though here the position is taken that this is not so, as has already been stated, the key being if we reverse the polarity and give pre-eminence to religion.

But if we return to the nineteenth century, various examples of archaeologists taking an interest in 'religious' aspects of their data can be found – for example, Christian Jürgensen Thomsen and Jens Worsaae, two Danish archaeologists who were instrumental in establishing the very discipline of archaeology in the mid-nineteenth century. Thomsen established the three-age system of stone, bronze, and iron for instance. Both Thomsen and Worsaae have been described by Bruce Trigger (1989: 86) as not only being interested in the technology and subsistence of past peoples but also in 'something about their social life and beliefs'.

Nevertheless, although archaeology was developing as a discipline in its own right, as attested by the examples just given, evolutionary approaches to religion which sometimes drew upon archaeological data were far from extinct, with the master of this approach being Sir James Frazer. His massive compendium, *The Golden Bough*, a work which has been described as 'quite impossible to summarise' (Sharpe 1986: 90), indicates this in the outline of his ideas of human progression from magic to religion to science. In effect, the presentation of pictures of religious advancement along a sliding scale of development, a process which he traces using primarily historical, ethnographic and anthropological evidence. Little archaeological evidence is, by contrast, drawn upon within Frazer's grand design. Though in the discussion of 'The Myth of Osiris', for example, we get references to the discovery and exploration of tombs of 'the most ancient kings of Egypt' at Abydos (Frazer 1936: 19). But essentially Frazer believed that if you have ethnography and anthropology you do not need archaeology, and was, overall, dismissive of prehistoric archaeology (Ucko 2001: 273).

Edward Burnett Tylor, in his *Religion in Primitive Culture* (1958), also developed a notion of three stages of social evolution: animism ('belief that a spirit or spirits is active in aspects of the environment' (Hinnells 1995: 41)); polytheism (belief in, or worship of, many gods); and monotheism (belief in, or worship of, one god) (Bowie 2000: 15). Animism was equated directly with 'stone age religion' and seen as something that was still extant in 'primitive' cultures (Sharpe 1986: 58). Direct analogies (see pp. 114–15) are used and prehistoric archaeology is called upon to support his theories of cultural advancement whereby 'primitive' forms such as 'the megalithic structures, menhirs, cromlechs, dolmens, and the like' of European prehistory are still found 'as matters of modern construction and recognized purpose among the ruder indigenous tribes of India' (Tylor 1929: vol. 1, 61).

Durkheim, though advocating a sociological definition of religion as already described, also approached his *Elementary Forms of Religious Life* (2001) through an evolutionary framework. He might have rejected animism and naturism and thus separated himself from Tylor or Max Müller, but as Cladis (2001: xvi) notes, his work reflected the ideology of the nineteenth century, 'the belief that the explanation of complex human phenomena requires the examination of their simpler, earlier forms'. Yet Durkheim's study is also brilliant in other respects, and cannot simply be discarded. One is his realisation that the search for the origins of religion, an absolute first beginning, must be dismissed as unachievable for 'like any human institution, religion begins nowhere' (Durkheim 2001: 9); this is an intuitive deduction that it would serve many well to acknowledge more fully today.

Evolutionary approaches can, rightly, be discarded as simplistic, reductionist, and in instances, racist. A posited sequence whereby a series of religious 'stages' is passed through is largely untenable. An example of such would usually involve a scheme in which shamanism could be described as largely the religion of hunter-gatherers because of the links with animals which recur, whereas ancestors as custodians of the land might grow more important with the growth of agriculture through being linked to cycles of fertility, seasonality and possession of the land (see Chapter 3). Then, increasing social stratification could be said to give rise to hierarchical religions involving priest castes/increased sacrifice/centralised control of resources. Finally, the historical dimension of literacy associated with a growth in universalising tendencies might be said to give rise to world religions.

Such a sequence is flawed, for the co-existence of different forms is evident – contrary to older approaches which ultimately saw the lower religions wiped out as they were replaced by higher ones. This is obviously not so; there are no universals. Similarly, the existence of a High or Sky God has to be admitted as existing amongst all these religious forms as well, something that might previously have been denied within an evolutionary schema. The sliding scale of religious evolution does not work; old gods can easily become new gods in an identity shift rather than a simple evolutionary step.

Other explicit archaeological approaches to religion are considered below, but it is important to reiterate that in terms of theoretical consideration it has largely been ignored. Hawkes's (1954) 'ladder' has already been mentioned as a rare example of the explicit consideration of archaeology and religion before the 1960s. Another instance which can be added is Grahame Clark's functionalist approach whereby different aspects of 'culture' such as economy, social and political organisation, and belief systems were studied in relation to each other as components of an overall functioning system. An approach which led Clark to conclude, as Trigger (1989: 265) notes, that 'when working only with archaeological data, archaeologists are likely to learn more about the economies of prehistoric societies than about their social organisation and religious beliefs'. This position with regard to archaeology and religion is all too evident in Clark's (1989) textbook *World Prehistory* whereby world religions as historically attested phenomena are more generously considered than traditional or prehistoric religions, and where these are treated this is usually with regard to 'concrete' evidence such as burials and pyramids.

## *Processual approaches: New Archaeology*

A wide range of material could be encompassed under the heading of processual archaeology, with the general processualist focus being, in the words of Pearson (2002: 2), 'an interest in explaining empirical observations about human behaviour by means of cross-cultural generalizations or laws and a conviction that these empirical observations (the archaeological data) are always independent of any theory'. In essence this provides a flawed perspective on the past in general, for in the words of Hodder (1988: 25, 26), individuals 'appear as predictable automata, driven by covering laws', and 'appear to be easily fooled'.

'New Archaeology', as exemplified by Binford's work, provides a useful example to focus upon. For credit for the explicit recognition that religion is a factor to be considered within archaeology, excluding those examples already referred to, has to be largely given to Lewis Binford. His systems approach included religion, for he believed that 'formal artefact assemblages and their contexts can yield a systematic and understandable picture of total extinct cultures' (Trigger 1989: 298). Within his paper 'Archaeology as Anthropology', Binford (1962: 218–19) refers to 'ideological sub-systems' and also what he calls 'ideotechnic artefacts' – items such as 'figures of deities, clan symbols, symbols of natural agencies etc.', described as having 'their primary functional context in the ideological component of the social system' (ibid.: 220, 219).

Yet although this recognition of religion (ideology) might have been made, at the same time it was discarded as 'epiphenomenal' (Whitley 1998: 9), and in reality the religious dimension was ignored. This was because, as Fritz (1978: 38) describes, endeavours at attempting to recover religion from archaeological data were defined as within the realms of 'palaeopsychology'. A correlate of Binford's argument, in the words of Bender *et al.* (1997: 148), is 'that what we had to worry about was what people *did*, not what they *thought*', with the net result being that 'the "new archaeology" was born with "ritual" as a little subsystem of a wider functioning whole' (ibid.).

If one analyses Binford's writings an overall neglect of religion is apparent. The 'big questions of archaeology' (1983: 26) might be asked of the origins of civilisation or agriculture, but the role of religion is not entertained. The volume, *In Pursuit of the Past* (Binford 1983) provides just such an example. Besides the theoretical lacunae regarding religion, its absence is also notice-able in the case studies considered. That concerning the Nunamiut of Anaktuvuk Pass, Alaska, for instance, where we learn much about the seasonal round, land use, site types, hunting and pro-cessing activities and patterns, but the impression is given that this was entirely carried out within a secular framework. In fact ethnography shows this to be flawed – although the definition of what it comprises is subject to debate (see Chapter 4), a shama-nistic system is the traditional religious universe within which Inuit beliefs are usually placed (see, for example, Vitebsky 1995: 106; Lowenstein 1993).

That Binford was aware of the fact that shamanism was impor-tant amongst the Nunamiut is apparent in his earlier volume, *Nunamiut Ethnoarchaeology*, where there is an explicit reference to 'powerful shamans' and a brief description provided of a 'shrine' (1978: 413, 427). Otherwise, however, religious aspects of Nunamiut life are not considered and instead Binford focuses upon 'behavioural variability' which has to be 'understood in purely pragmatic terms' (ibid.: 414). This is a theme which is continued in Binford's portrayal of the Alaskan Inuit within *In Pursuit of the Past*, with kill-sites, butchering sites, hunting stands, storage sites, and 'lovers'' camps even, all described in detail; but shrines, sacred places, the possible ambivalent identity of some of the site types already mentioned, are all ignored.

Overall this is a glaring omission, as Vitebsky, for instance, refers to the *inukshuk* – 'stones piled in human shape to control the movements of caribou' – used by Inuit groups (1995: 106). In a functionalist-type paradigm as adopted by Binford these might be considered perhaps as hunting decoys when in reality they belong within the frame of reference whereby 'a shaman may be able to locate or lure game because he or she has actually been a game animal' (ibid.: 106); a functional interpretation thereby proving not wholly applicable. Equally, the very notion of the hunt is not a secular activity but seemingly embedded within Nunamiut religious belief for the concept of a 'caribou mother' exists, who 'requires the traditional observances con-cerning hunting on land' (Merkur 1991: 90). Therefore the very activity itself, the hunt, as described by Binford, could be described as inappropriately defined. Such an approach can be juxtaposed with Soviet studies of related peoples where although religion might be denigrated or misinterpreted at least it is acknowledged (see, for example, Hutton (2001) for a discussion of such issues).

Another example is provided by Binford's (1972a) study of red ochre use at four sites in Michigan: Huron Beach, Pomranky, Kimmel and Eastport, all dating from between circa 1400–300 BCE. At Huron Beach, for example, 67 stone points were found 'in a tight cluster, covered with powdered red ochre and in association with human bone' (ibid.: 301–2). This is exactly the sort of material which could be considered within a religious/ritual framework; instead it is tested, analysed, and compared, between site and within site, in terms of cultural drift, a model used to explain change in cultural elements such as social organisation and demography. But an attempt at reconstructing the overall meaning of the burials and their grave goods in religious, ritual, or even symbolic terms is not attempted. Instead, Binford outlines how he hopes that the burial 'ceremonialism' might ultimately be evaluated, this being an empty term which fits in with the general avoidance of 'religion' as an explanatory label other than as a broadly defined philosophical category briefly discussed in relation to the general study of mortuary practices (Binford 1972b: 209–13).

David Clarke's (1978: 101–2) analytical archaeology, by contrast, acknowledges religion more fully as an aspect of human behaviour amenable to archaeological investigation but treats it as a subsystem of the overall socio-cultural system, with others being the social, psychological, economic and material culture subsystems. Religion is described as communicative and 'constraining the activities of individuals in most societies' (ibid.: 110), and also, rightly, as 'speculative and broad' (ibid.: 112). Although at least acknowledging something of the complexities of religion and its archaeological investigation, religion need not, as described, be a subsystem, but instead can form the very system itself into which his other 'subsystems' would fit.

Equally, Fritz (1978), already mentioned as criticising Binford for his maligning of the investigation of the archaeology of religions as somehow a fringe activity, approaches the archaeology of religion from a processually rule-bound perspective. Religion is subsumed within 'ideational systems' (ibid.: 39) which are said to be manifest through 'sets of rules' evident materially, through architecture for instance, something he attempts to prove with a case study based around material dating from the ninth to twelfth/thirteenth centuries CE from Chaco Canyon in the US. In effect, universal claims are made, but claims which are in turn related to very local case studies. Another, and important contribution to processual approaches to the archaeology of religion was made by Colin Renfrew (1985), but this is considered later within the framework of cognitive processualism, which Renfrew's work helped give rise to.

Alternatively, and also within a processual framework, science might be seen as offering a mechanism for beginning to understand the archaeology of religion. Brian Fagan's book, *From Black Land to Fifth Sun*, for example, emphasises modern science as a means of approaching 'the intangible' (1998: 8). Defined religious/ritual sites such as Stonehenge or Çatal Hüyük are the dominant focus of discussion, and belief is made tangible through focusing upon such concrete categories of religious site, allied with the application of scientific techniques such as Geographical Information Systems (GIS), described as having 'enormous, and still largely unrealized potential for the study of sacred places and ancient landscapes' (ibid.: 14).

This might be true, but similarly it is not a panacea. GIS has to be initiated by someone, and the variables which will actually form its system, its fields of analysis and the categories of information recorded, have to be decided. These boundaries of analysis are thus not scientifically 'neutral', nor the solution which the archaeology of religion might demand; scientific enquiry need not be suppressed, but the techniques which it encompasses form only a minor part of the general armoury which can be employed. Furthermore, scientific techniques can equally be misused and 'science' be ignored or misinterpreted if its results do not necessarily fit with what the investigator desired, especially where religious belief and an emphasis upon proof might be concerned, and examples of this are considered later.

## Marxist approaches

Marxist perspectives on religion are not neutral, perhaps unsurprisingly, and in general Marxist-Leninist principles on religion have been described by Basilov (1984: 56) as defining it as 'a form of social consciousness'. The foreword to the Russian edition of Marx and Engel's *On Religion* (Anon 1972) indicates this perfectly. Besides applying the doctrine that religion was used 'as an opiate for the popular masses' (ibid.: 7), the claim is also made that 'Marxism alone was able completely to reveal the essence of religion' (ibid.: 8), whilst famously Marx himself refers to religion as 'the sigh of the oppressed creature' (Marx and Engels 1972: 38). Hence in following the subsequent definition of the 'task of history' (ibid.), archaeology, as in part a sister discipline to history, could be ascribed a role in establishing 'the truth of this world' (ibid.) including the false consciousness which is religion (from a Marxist perspective).

Within archaeology, a classic example of the adoption of a Marxist perspective on the past, including past beliefs, is provided by the work of Gordon Childe (1945, 1947, 1956). In *Progress and Archaeology* (Childe 1945: 78), for instance, a pessimistic position is adopted with regard to what can be recovered of human 'spiritual experiences', but at least Childe acknowledges there are these dimensions which archaeologists can investigate, if they are related to what he terms the 'deed' (burials, sacrifices and temples). Childe recognises the importance of religion, albeit from a negative perspective, with, overall, religion seen as functioning as a delusion, in perpetuating 'theocratic despotism' (Childe 1947: 73) – i.e. classic Marxism – yet he also realises that 'utility is not the only value admitted by any society' (Childe 1956: 43). In other words, further dimensions to the human condition exist. Equally, some of the universals taken for granted in interpreting the past are also questioned by Gordon Childe:

reason, agency and logic (ibid.: 169), for instance. It is admitted that these vary according to 'culture', an important point with regard to the archaeology of religion, as already discussed.

But in general, in Marxist approaches to archaeology religion is frequently subsumed within ideology (Miller and Tilley 1984), and the role of ideology in turn, as Hodder (1988: 61) notes, 'is determined by and functions in relation to the economy'. Ideology itself has been described by Parker Pearson (1982: 100) as 'remarkably hard to define', though his attempt at this describes ideology 'as a system of beliefs through which the perceived world of appearances is interpreted as a concrete and objectified reality'. This is a less rigorous definition than that provided by Shanks and Tilley (1982: 130) who argue that ideology is a 'practice which operates to secure the reproduction of relations of dominance and to conceal contradictions between the structural principles orientating the actions of individuals and groups within the social formation'. This would appear to be more of a pure Marxist definition, later summarised by Parker Pearson (1984: 60) as involving a concept of ideology as '"false consciousness" (and a set of beliefs which distort the true nature of social relations) and that, since the material conditions of life determine consciousness, ideology is the product of human action in the world'. A second sense of ideology in Marxism is an understanding of reality that emerges from the lived experience of a particular group or class (J. Thomas, pers. comm.; see also McGuire 1992).

Applied case studies involving archaeology and ideology (religion), as approached from a Marxist position, are varied (McGuire 1992), though those concerned with the sphere of funerary archaeology are more frequent (e.g. Parker Pearson 1982). Shanks and Tilley (1982) for example, in examining skeletal evidence from various neolithic barrows in Southern Sweden, and in Wessex and the Cotswolds in England, conduct their analysis by 'adopting the conception of ritual as a form of ideology, and the skeleton as a non-arbitrary symbolic set'. Thus here, ritual also equals ideology, again reflecting the lack of definition evident in Marxist archaeological philosophy as regards religion (and in Marxist philosophy in general), a point which is returned to again later (see pp. 78–9).

But not all archaeologists working within a Marxist framework necessarily avoid using the terms 'ritual' and 'religion'. Kristiansen (1984) uses both in his comparative examination of megalithic and single-grave cultures in neolithic and Bronze Age Denmark. Though his conclusion that the megalithic culture 'linked subsistence, social organisation and religion very closely to one another in a ritualised vertical structure of reproduction', whereas the single-grave culture 'separated these institutions, being dominated by a competitive horizontal social structure of alliances and exchange, based on local economic autonomy' (ibid.: 85), Kristiansen could be accused of leaving little room for the individual – itself reflecting the further Marxist view that, as Kus (1984: 105) notes, it 'does not necessarily demand the identification of individuals'.

Today, however, Marxist archaeological approaches, as with Marxism in general, are of little consequence and are part of the history of our discipline, hence their consideration being placed within this chapter. However, in the often-cyclical nature of interpretative fashion they could, of course, again become important.

## *Far-fetched and direct analogy approaches: 'prehistoric religion'*

The opposite of the neglect of religion within archaeology is provided by research where the interpretation of archaeological material is taken to sometimes far-fetched extremes. Older archaeological research considering 'prehistoric religion' frequently reflects such a process, and often this was completed by drawing simple analogies from ethnographic material and then directly transferring this onto the past. Eliade, for example, calls for an understanding of 'homo religiosus' to be obtained, in part, through analogy with 'primitive societies' (1959: 165), so that 'studying the rural societies of Europe provides some basis for understanding the religious world of the Neolithic cultivators' (ibid.: 164). Similar simplistic use of analogy is suggested for the palaeolithic where it is argued that Arctic hunters share the same economy as palaeolithic peoples and thus 'very probably the same religious ideology. . . . Hence, comparison of prehistoric documents with ethnological facts is justified' (Eliade 1979: 15).

Other scholars such as Narr (1964) recognise that the use of ethnographic analogy for interpreting 'prehistoric religion' was more complex than that just described. He acknowledges, for instance, in referring to links between contemporary 'primitives' and the palaeolithic, that 'a number of constants of human nature and behaviour' exist, but that to make the use of analogy successful, relying upon singular similarities which appear infrequently is not the way to achieve this. Rather, we can 'only use those which occur in sufficient breadth and accord' to allow inferences to be made (ibid.: 13). This is a fair point, and the use of analogy is considered in greater detail in Chapter 4. However, others are less cautious in its theoretical conception and practical application.

The interpretation of the existence of a 'cave bear cult' in parts of Europe in the middle palaeolithic provides a cogent example. Maringer (1960: 28), for instance, describes how at Drachenloch Cave in the Swiss Alps, within a part of the cave interpreted as a living area, a low wall constructed of limestone slabs of some 60 cm height had been built, with the gap between this wall and the cave wall 'a veritable store of cave-bear bones'. This accumulation of cave bear remains included several skulls similarly oriented, whilst in another part of the cave elements of a four further cave bears had been assembled. The presence of these remains was linked to their becoming a focus of religious belief due to their being derived from an animal the hunters feared and respected which 'they honoured by sacrifice' (ibid.: 42), as a sort of Lord of the Beasts perhaps. Ethnographic analogy was used to support this theory variously derived from 'Caucasian mountain peoples whose environment is similar to that of the old cave bear hunters' (ibid.: 34), as well as the Ainu of Japan and the Tungus of Siberia. A comparable interpretation for the Drachenloch evidence is proposed later by Burl (1981: 22).

Needless to say, and as touched upon earlier, the evidence for such formalised ritual practices or religious beliefs within the middle palaeolithic is far from convincing. With the Drachenloch material taphonomy would appear to be a major factor. Gargett (1989) has questioned the shape, size and contents of the stone 'cysts' of the type formed by the limestone wall described previously, with the concentration of bear crania suggested as the result of natural processes rather than a middle palaeolithic cave bear cult. Chase and Dibble (1987: 277) describe how the factual presentation of the Drachenloch evidence has altered over time so that originally one cave bear skull had the proximal end of a femur passing through the left zygomatic arch of the skull, which in later descriptions transmuted into its passing through the right arch!

The alternative to the simplistic use of ethnographic analogy in reconstructing 'prehistoric religion' is interpretation which allows the imagination to run wild, and again examples can be drawn from European prehistory by way of illustrating such approaches. The cave of El Juyo 8 km west of Santander in Spain was the focus of excavation in the late 1970s during which what has been interpreted as a sanctuary complex radiocarbon dated to $c$. 14,000 years ago was uncovered (Freeman and González Echegaray 1981). A structure composed of numerous layers and deposits of material was excavated. This included fill layers of sand, earth and clay, some arranged in 'rosettes', as well as horizons of burnt vegetation, animal remains (as well as deer feet and ribs placed in their natural position) and ochre. The resulting mound was encased in a clay 'shell' reinforced with stone slabs and animal long bones. Further circular pits were also recorded. These contained eyed bone needles, ochre, limpet and periwinkle shells, as well as a 'channel of communication' lined with 'black, greasy earth' which connected the mound just described to another smaller structure (ibid.: 8–9). The description of this structure by Freeman and González Echegaray (1981) is perfectly adequate, and the summary just provided fails to convey its complexity. However, it is in the interpretation of this material, and especially that provided to account for a stone 'face' said to be presiding over the sanctuary that fault can be found (Figure 3).

First, the stone 'face', interpreted as depicting a semi-human face with moustache, lips, teeth, a smiling mouth, and eyes all

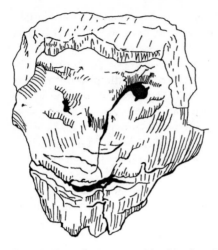

*Figure 3* 'Stone face' or natural boulder from El Juyo

*Source:* After Freeman and González Echegaray (1981: 12)

rendered, can be questioned as nothing of the sort; that it is merely a stone bearing natural marks and contours which has been circumstantially placed where it was found in the cave, perhaps due to taphonomic action, is possible. Second, and more fundamentally, Freeman and González Echegaray move from this questionable piece of evidence to make some far-fetched claims. For example, the face becomes 'a supernatural being' representing on one side an adult human and on the other a lion or leopard, which Jungian 'depth psychology' suggests was a 'graphic representation' of the integration of the savage and the controlled 'during the individuation process' (1981: 18). The channel with its greasy deposit, described previously as linking the smaller structure to the interior of the larger, becomes 'the symbolic expression of a new and maturer emotional orientation towards the 'secrets' of reproduction' (ibid.). Now these might on the one hand be exciting interpretations which offer a far-sighted insight into upper palaeolithic religious practices denied to the majority of archaeologists, but alternatively they might not, and here, unfortunately, it seems that the latter analysis is more relevant for the simple reason that the jump from the evidence to the interpretation is seemingly unsupported by the data, and hence the reading that is offered is best termed as 'far-fetched' in its dramatic claims.

Another example is provided by the work of Gimbutas (1989, 1996), which although compared by Campbell (1989: xiii) in its significance to that of François Champollion and his deciphering of the Rosetta Stone, is placed within this section because of its literal claims to having interpreted the role of the 'Goddess' in prehistoric religion. Essentially, Gimbutas traces her Goddess back to the upper palaeolithic in its main elements: 'the mystery of birth and death and the renewal of life' (Gimbutas 1989: xix), as represented in the first sculptures of bone and ivory incised with symbols such as vulvas and breasts. This reaches fruition in the Goddess world of Old Europe, a period of pre-Indo-European culture, 'matrifocal and probably matrilineal, agricultural and sedentary, egalitarian and peaceful' (Gimbutas 1996: 9). An era brought to an end by the Indo-European associated Kurgan (burial mound) culture which was linked in opposition with 'patriarchy' and 'patrilineality' (Gimbutas 1989: xx), as well as animal husbandry, small-scale agriculture and the importance of weapons.

These are ideas which have been remarkably pervasive and long-lasting; indeed, they have influenced the perceptions of some visitors to the site of Çatal Hüyük in Turkey, described in the next chapter. But likewise they are not without their detractors in what can be a much-polarised area of debate (see, for example, Meskell 1995; Haaland and Haaland 1995). Without repeating the extensive criticisms which have already been exhaustively levelled at Gimbutas's theories, a primary weakness, if anything, is the basic fact that rather than 'a single, fundamental pattern universally repeating itself' (Goodison and Morris 1998: 16) the picture of Goddess form and importance is really one of 'plurality' (ibid.) and complexity. Equally, there is no 'firm evidence' (Tringham and Conkey 1998: 39) for the Kurgan invasions and their terminating the era of 'figurines and matrilocal harmony' (ibid.). In summary, Gimbutas's theories and 'language' of the

Goddess are too simplistic and too clear-cut to account for such a range of material spread over such a broad period of time.

Other more recent manifestations of 'far-fetched' interpretations are those which attribute the appearance of shamanism everywhere. For example, Strassburg (2000: abstract) has approached shamanism within the southern Scandinavian mesolithic (c. 7000–4000 BCE) from a 'cyborgian' theoretical perspective described as 'an elaborate mix of queer theory, feminism, archaeology, anthropology, and philosophy'. The end result, rather than achieving his 'critical theoretical cyborg' (ibid.: 4), is to produce a piece of work which might be fashionable but is insubstantial. Shamanism might be 'queered', but Strassburg is still, it could be argued, applying an orthodox definition, 'shamanism', which is problematic in itself (see Chapter 4) and thus in reality does little in exploring the undoubted complexities of religion in southern Scandinavia during the mesolithic. To this could be added shamanic attributions for ley lines (Devereux 2001), or the protracted debate surrounding various interpretations of shaman-associated, altered states of consciousness (trance) derived rock art – as, for example, that surrounding engravings within neolithic passage tombs such as Newgrange or Knowth in Ireland (Dronfield 1996; Bahn 1996).

Further manifestations of such approaches exist (see, for example, Lissner 1961; Maringer 1977, 1979). These are to be commended in admitting a religious dimension within prehistoric material, but here the swing is in the opposite direction often manifest in the transference of modern religious labels and classifications onto inappropriate material. Thus, for example, Maringer (1977) posits the existence of priests/priestesses in the neolithic based upon the existence of certain preconditions, such as:

- A differentiated economy with a settled way of life.
- Leisure for spiritual activities.
- A production surplus.
- 'Material foundation of rich sacrificial custom requiring special ritual members' (ibid.: 101).
- The existence of centres requiring priests/priestesses.

Besides the inappropriacy of universal checklists, for which exceptions can always be found, rendering such neat schemes invalid, the primary problem lies in the search for defined 'religion' within prehistory – meaning religion as conceived of within an ordered hierarchical system with priests, sanctuaries and 'adorants' (Maringer 1979), and though examples have not been found, perhaps bishops and cathedrals as well. (Similar problems can be suggested for 'shamans', 'animists', 'totems', etc. and this is considered further in Chapter 4.) In other words, modern conceptions projected back onto material to which we might be able to ascribe the term 'religious', but which eludes by its very nature further refining according to a limited range of labels which remain little considered but are applied as 'givens'.

## Other approaches

Various other approaches have been employed within the archaeological study of religion, predominantly with regard to world religions. These approaches, which are largely methodological rather than theoretical, have been reviewed elsewhere in some detail (Insoll 2001b), and again it is unnecessary to repeat this here. However, two brief examples follow.

### Art-historical, architectural and checklist-type approaches

Within the art-historical approach there is an absence of theoretical rationale as to why the research is being completed, and archaeology functions predominantly as a provider or verifier of works of art, or as an object of discussion within the framework of iconographic debate. Emphasis will be placed upon iconography and symbolism, but within a particularist perspective whereby this becomes the driving force behind archaeological research. Numerous examples of such a type of approach being employed exist, and to single out any scholars' work in particular is not to detract from the worthiness of such research.

Hachlili (1999) provides a cogent example within her study of the 'Hand of God' in ancient Near Eastern, Jewish and Early

Christian art. Here, much of the material considered derives from archaeological contexts, but emphasis is lent to one particular facet of the evidence: the treatment is largely descriptive and the resultant conclusions very specific. Alternatively, religious architectural data recovered from archaeological contexts may form the focus of attention, but it will be similarly treated, perhaps as the focus of a particular architectural question – its relation to a particular architectural style or typology for instance (see Rodwell (1989) for a critique of such approaches within the context of church archaeology). Yet the end result in terms of audience for the work, fit of the body of data within its overall context, and theoretical rationale (or rather, absence thereof) is the same.

Equally theoretically devoid are what could be termed 'checklist' approaches which have been sometimes employed within the archaeological study of religion. These are not to be confused with the types of holistic approaches described earlier (for example, Insoll 1999a). Instead, checklists differ significantly as this is literally what they are: a supposed procedure for the archaeological recognition of religion by ticking the relevant boxes. This is something Lane (2001: 150) has recently considered with reference to the recognition of Christianity in Roman Britain, where he makes the relevant point that 'while checklists can prove helpful in the task of interpreting particular archaeological contexts, they rarely, if ever, have universal applicability'. In this particular instance meaning that, for example, the recognition of Christian burial within a Romano-British context by east–west alignment, and an absence of accompanying grave goods, is far from universally assured, contrary to earlier approaches (Radford 1971).

## In search of proof

Approaches to the archaeology of religions which are dictated by the search for proof for (or attempts to disprove) religious events, texts, figures and artefacts have also figured prominently, frequently accompanied by much controversy, and these have been considered by this author elsewhere with particular reference to biblical archaeology (Insoll 2001b: 10–15). It was described how within biblical archaeology it is possible to chart over time the changing use of archaeology as a means of proving or disproving biblical events, usually, but not solely, with a Christian focus. Although today biblical archaeology might have been largely subsumed within Near Eastern archaeology, and thus could be said to be evincing a rationale defined by Silberman (1998: 185) as 'devoted to the archaeological excavation of the lands of the Bible without being committed, as an institution, to any particular religious understanding, national interest or historical ideology', this has not always been so.

According to Yamauchi (1972), archaeology began to be used in biblical studies on a large scale as a reaction to the biblical criticism prevalent in the latter half of the nineteenth century, especially in Germany as exemplified by the Tübingen School. Such overt approaches to the use of archaeology as a means of furnishing texts, combating criticism, and making scriptures 'better respected' (Unger 1962: 26) were frequently driven by fideistic perspectives, a term already introduced, and defined by Hinnells (1995: 170) as stressing 'the primary role of the commitment of faith in providing the basis for theological understanding'. Yamauchi (1972: 26), for example, mentions that his book is 'written by one who is committed to the historical Christian faith, seeks to summarise, albeit in selective fashion, the archaeological evidence and its bearings upon the Scriptures'. This emphasis upon selectivity is a problematical feature; emphasis upon proof might be evident, but if the evidence contradicts the asserted viewpoint then it is just discounted.

A classic example of such perspective in action is provided by the highly polarised research surrounding the Turin Shroud. From a believer's perspective this is the shroud of Christ miraculously imprinted with a sepia image of the full figure of a man, including wounds and stigmata. Yet when this was subjected to C14 dating at three different laboratories, and the results indicated a date of *c*. 1260–1390, i.e. from the medieval period (Bortin 1980), this evidence was discounted as unnecessary or inaccurate by those who believe in the artefact. Hoare (1994: 98, 105–6), for instance, attempts to dismantle the results of the radiocarbon dating, citing adulteration of the shroud as the result of a fire, atmospheric pollutants, or something inherent in the production of the linen for example. Alternatively, as Picknett and Prince (1994: 176) note, believers counter evidence such as that of the C14 date by reasoning that 'this is the Son of God . . . , and therefore the laws of Nature may well have been altered, speeded up, slowed down or suspended altogether'; in other words, belief in divine action.

Such approaches to the archaeology of religion, as driven by faith and with an emphasis upon furnishing proof, are certainly not unique to biblical archaeology of a Christian slant, but they are more common, perhaps reflecting, in part, the longer history of relevant archaeological research. With regard to Judaism for example, such studies are usually also classified within biblical archaeology, but they certainly exist (Whitelam 1996). Similarly so within Hinduism, where, for example, the great Hindu epic, the *Mahabharata*, has been the focus of archaeological study (Chakrabarti 1999; Lad 1983). Equally, radical Hinduism and archaeology have collided, so to speak, in the events surrounding the demolition of the Ayodhya mosque, and the subsequent sectarian violence. Briefly summarised, this involved a mosque dating from the sixteenth century being pulled down in 1992 as it was thought to have been built upon the birthplace of Rama, the Hindu god and king. The support for this act was partially provided by archaeological interpretation, the merits of which have been questioned. Rao (1999: 46) describes how in the original excavation report nothing of significance linked with any Rama temple at Ayodhya was discussed; but later this was changed and a claim made 'that evidence of a temple had in fact been found' (ibid., and see Mandal 1993).

Some archaeological research focusing on sites and events associated with Buddha has also been completed in Nepal and India (for discussion, see Coningham 2001: 65–70). In contrast, the Qur'an, though the focus of various historical studies (e.g. Wansbrough 1977; Crone 1987), has not been the target of archaeological approaches driven by a search for proof, one reason being from a Muslim believer's perspective that, 'the truth is already revealed and material culture, and therefore archaeology, cannot confirm or deny the faith of believers' (Insoll 1999a: 231). This said, archaeology has been used from a Muslim perspective for a variety of purposes, including reviewing 'past societies that have been destroyed because of their rebellion against Allah' (Yahya 2001: 4), as recorded in the Qur'an. These are further described (ibid.) as being '"observable" and "identifiable" thanks to the current archive studies and archaeological finds', so that we get, for example, discussion of the archaeological evidence correlating with Nuh's (Noah's) flood in Mesopotamia, or that interpreted as attesting to the destruction of Sodom, or the people of Lut as they are referred to in the Qur'an, and situated, according to Yahya (ibid.: 41) 'in the area of the Dead Sea which stretches along the Israel–Jordan border'.

Outside of world religious contexts, such an emphasis upon finding proof is largely absent, though it could be suggested that some of the vocabulary used within archaeology focused upon the investigation of shamanism appears to veer in this direction, or is at least is seemingly dictated by what might otherwise be referred to as fideistic perspectives (see Chapter 1) couched under a 'neo-shamanic' or 'new age' label. Hence, for example, Wallis argues that his

> fledgling 'experential anthropology' challenges those anthropologists concerned with going native to alter their view. Their fear is a colonialist hangover, a fear of descent into 'savagery'. Experential anthropology deconstructs the paradigm of absolute 'objectivity' and 'detachment', and replaces them with the nuanced understandings the 'insider's' view can bring.
>
> (Wallis 2001: 214)

Now, difficulties with achieving an 'insider's' perspective aside (see p. 39), a primary problem with such perspectives is that those who disagree are accused of 'shamanophobia' (Wallis and Lymer 2001: xiii), and thus the useful points made regarding alternative views on the past, which are rightly promoted by proponents of such an approach as having validity, are somewhat subsumed in the creation of a 'shamanic archaeology' rather than an 'archaeology of shamanism' – the former analogous with an 'Islamic archaeology', or a 'biblical archaeology', which tends toward a highly vociferous 'pro' stance, with counter voices treated almost as dissension. But equally it is perhaps partly a product of the polarised extent of much of the debate within the archaeology of shamanism (see Chapter 4), where critics of the approach, likewise unhelpfully, have introduced the term 'shamaniacs' (Bahn 2001: 81) to refer to their opponents. Nonetheless, this said, the questioning of supposed archaeological credentials of 'objectivity and impartiality', which for example Wallis (2001: 214) suggests needs addressing, is to be commended, for archaeologists' sometimes presumed hold on 'ancient' religions is not a birthright of our vocation.

# 3

# CONTEMPORARY APPROACHES

Contemporary approaches to the archaeology of religion are equally varied and again only a selection can be considered here. These differ according to which chronological period or geographical area is being studied, frequently with little cross-over: cognitive processualism in researching the upper palaeolithic, or post-processual-linked phenomenology applied to the neolithic. This also certainly seems to be true of the religious 'forms' allowed for in European prehistory, where the obsession with classification critiqued previously means that we have bounded entities proposed for each chronological period.

Within the framework of European prehistory, for example, shamans people the religious worlds of the upper palaeolithic (Lewis-Williams 2002), and likewise the mesolithic (Zvelebil 1997: 42–4), whereas the European neolithic is characterised by the proliferation of ancestor cults usually described as being of communal orientation. In the Bronze Age the appearance of notions of personhood are inferred, with the recognition of the individual interpreted as a factor in religious belief, and often again centred on ancestor worship. However, whether these divisions reflect the true systems of beliefs in these periods is uncertain; everything appears a little too clear cut and tidy, and the 'messy' edges surrounding complex phenomena such as religion are largely absent.

With regard to the European neolithic the picture of religious 'orthodoxy', as presented, has been criticised by James Whitley (2002: 119) who has made the point that 'ancestors are everywhere, and everything is ancestral'. Undeniably the ancestors, and possible accompanying ties to the land, grew in importance with the origins of agriculture, but equally we should not seek to explain in a mono-explanatory way what was probably a complex system of beliefs. Neolithic religion is here seemingly being categorised using modern religious labels applied in the singular when perhaps it was composed of multiple elements of which ancestor cults only formed a part, and which were not necessarily always present anyway.

## The parts do not equal a whole: particularistic approaches

Aspects of archaeological evidence often associated with religion, such as funerary remains, have been the focus of a great deal of contemporary archaeological study. In contrast, other categories of evidence of relevance to the archaeological study of religion have been much more neglected, those pertaining to gender or diet for example. This is in part a reflection of the survival of evidence. Tombs and other funerary remains frequently survive and are very visible, whereas animal bones and seeds might also survive but are often less visible and perceived as more difficult to recover. Alternatively, where they are recovered they will frequently be treated within an economic framework, whilst interpretations of gender, where considered, are similarly usually generated within a secular paradigm. Equally, this skewing of research is simply also a reflection of people's fascination with death as opposed to diet or gender. Yet in total it is also an indication of the absence of the type of holistic approach that the effective archaeological study of religion requires, as was outlined earlier (see pp. 22–3). Particularism is given precedence over a more complete understanding, even where the evidence might allow a fuller evaluation.

## *Death*

Hence, contrary to Hegel's notion that 'history is the record of what man does with the dead', as recounted by Oestigaard (1999: 345), the concern within this study is not with funerary archaeology. Why? First, death is not the sum total of religion. The view that 'death is the pivot round which religious thinking invariably revolves' (Chaudhuri 1997: 152) might be partially correct, but it is simplistic to assume that this is necessarily the be all and end all of religious belief, doctrine and philosophy. Dealing with death is not solely the reason why religions exist, but this fact is often neglected and hence religion as a force within life beyond concerns with mortality and the afterlife is ignored. Second, for the simple reason that it is one area of relevance to the archaeology of religions which has been intensively examined from a whole gamut of perspectives (for review, see for example, Parker Pearson 1999; Taylor 2002). This includes, besides the numerous regional and chronological studies of death in all its dimensions relating to all aspects of death and burial – sacrifice, cremation, grave goods, palaeopathology, etc. (see, for example, Campbell and Green 1995; Oestigaard 1999, 2000b; Downes and Pollard 1999) – the application and exploration of all types of theoretical approaches.

These range from those built upon a grand scale – as exemplified by Parker Pearson's (2001: 215) approach towards the 'human experience of death' undertaken with reference to the growth of monumentality, the quest for 'immortality' and the development of world religions which is neo-evolutionary in tone – to those of much more local significance. Alternatively, there are processual-type approaches, of secular emphasis, which might see treatment after death bearing some degree of predictable relationship with status in life, manifest, for instance, in a correlation between the existence of elaborate graves and the former degree of social differentiation evident (O'Shea 1984). This, it is usually argued following such a chain of logic, is something which can be charted through presumed regularities in mortuary practice, and through the application of ethnographic analogy as a source of inference.

Thus also of relevance to our brief review here are the cautionary tales which exist and which expose such presumed life–death correlations and regularities to be far from uniform. Peter Ucko (1969), for instance, highlights classic examples of the pitfalls which await the unwary archaeologist casually applying ethnographic analogy to the funerary record.

Yet, as will be considered in greater detail in Chapter 4, it is undeniable that ethnographic analogy can provide a wealth of possibilities in broadening interpretative horizons, including those pertaining to death and its archaeological correlates. Terje Oestigaard's (1999, 2000a) research on funerary rituals among Hindu communities in Nepal and India provides a cogent recent example, as his work on sacrifice and cremation indicates both the complexities which can exist and those that could potentially underpin the archaeological material with which we are concerned. Based upon ethnographic observation, he argues that cremations can be viewed as ritual transformations in that distinctions evident between those who are cremated and then buried and those who are buried in inhumations alone are in turn related to social status achieved through life-cycle rituals (Oestigaard 1999: 358). Such observations are then drawn upon in helping interpret Norwegian funerary material dating from the Late Bronze Age through to the Late Iron Age. As, for example, in suggesting that the use of food utensils and vessels as containers for the ashes of the deceased is possibly significant in strengthening his theory of ritual transformation, as manifest in cremation rites; that is, that 'the irreversibility of food transformations has its parallel in the irreversibility of the crossing and re-creation of boundaries: death becomes life again in terms of survival as ancestors' (ibid.: 359). Potential complexity is signalled and death is firmly 'locked' into life.

The act of *sati*, or widow-burning, formerly found in India (albeit comparatively rarely, contra the stereotypes), provides a further related example which indicates how this funerary related self-immolation is potentially linked into many spheres of life, rather than functioning as a 'stand-alone' action divorced from the wider social and religious whole. *Sati* is an immensely complex act, being an expression of individualism *in extremis*, but also of union as well, with the 'burning as two halves of a symbiotic whole, both husband and wife go to an imagined invisible world' (Menski 2002: 397–8). Besides potentially expunging the 'powerfully symbolic negative load (Fuller 1992: 23) of widowhood, perhaps also its meaning could be extended symbolically to the further dimension of family and community level significance in that through consigning herself to her husband's funerary pyre, the *sati* becomes the mediator of potential family/community shame, if anything engendered through her not completing the action of self-sacrifice. Oestigaard (2003: 16) considers this with regard to the notion of the 'sacrificial death', and describes how when a widow 'tried to escape, the relatives forced her back on the pyre – into the fire'. In this respect the correlation which Fuller (1992: 23) describes between high caste and the practice of *sati* must also be of significance, again in maintaining status and purity. Thus the individual immolation assumes a power beyond that of the individual alone.

In consequence, potentially, through bearing such examples in mind, the urn or post-hole filled with burnt bone could take on a new significance as the remains of an action linked into a much wider frame of reference than the immediate death-related context itself. Of course, such an inference will remain at the level of a suggestion alone, but by forming links between the different facets of archaeological evidence it might be possible to embed funerary data within a potential 'whole'. However, it can be suggested that much of the ethnographic data utilised by archaeologists in interpreting funerary remains within, for example, European prehistory, comes from a limited range of contexts, thereby limiting interpretative horizons from the outset anyway. A prime example of this is provided by the Merina of Madagascar, with their multi-stage burial practices, who recur frequently as a source of analogy for interpreting neolithic chambered tombs in parts of Britain or France for instance (see Scarre (1994) for relevant discussion).

Overall, the degree of acknowledgement of religion within the archaeological study of death and burial obviously varies immensely – from a position of complete neglect, with funerary treatment seen predominantly as a secular concern related perhaps to social or political considerations, as noted, through to other studies which focus upon religion as a potential structuring agent for the treatment of the dead. Parker Pearson (1999, 2001), for example, chosen as a brief focus here because of his undoubted contributions within this area of archaeology, acknowledges the role of religion but links it within his self-stated position that, 'spiritual beliefs have social and material conditions and, as such, are historically contingent. Organised religion is neither a necessary nor an eternal element of human spirituality' (2001: 217). A position influenced by a hint of Marxism perhaps, but certainly one which it can be suggested results in the creation of a metanarrative, to misuse a term introduced later on, whereby religion, death and society march hand in hand, but equally a narrative which is presented as devoid of spirituality, or mystery, elements which do (and have), undeniably, underpin many people's comprehension of death.

In this respect the important point to return to is the recurrent lack of a holistic perspective which might allow broad interpretations to be tested more rigorously. But to treat funerary archaeology on its own, as a means to an end in itself is, inevitably, to weaken the interpretative outcomes. The archaeology of death is frequently influenced by religious belief but forms a part of the overall framework. Here ethnography, a major source of evidence which is drawn upon to help interpret archaeological funerary data as already described, can be used to provide just such an insight into the potential existing myopic nature of much analysis completed. This observation is provided by Mircea Eliade (1978b: 37) in describing the symbolism of the funerary ceremonies among the Kogi of Colombia, whilst in so doing he makes the point that the external observer would be hard-pressed to understand what they meant without a comprehension of the totality of religious belief involved. In other words, the parts would not be understood without some insight into the whole, and it can be

suggested that this is a far from unique example. Within archaeology, admittedly, reconstructing the totality of prehistoric religion is an unachievable ideal rightly long since abandoned, but
the prominence accorded funerary data, when other facets of the
evidence could be integrated where available, is particularist
and indicative of what has already been referred to as the part(s)
not equalling a whole.

## *Animal remains and diet*

In contrast, diet and the study of animal remains are neglected
areas in the archaeology of religion but ones of critical importance
in creating and maintaining religious identities through, for
instance, the recognition of dietary laws, food taboos and pro-
hibitions, the use of food and animals in sacrifices and offerings,
and their similar utilisation in feasts, fasts and festivals (see, for
example, Simoons 1994). Reasons of space preclude a detailed
examination of this topic, and focus is accordingly drawn in
upon faunal remains alone, but even within this area of study
research has concentrated upon issues such as herd management
strategies, animal exploitation patterns and the use of secondary
products to the detriment of the consideration of possible
religious or symbolic reasoning which could similarly structure
animal exploitation, and thus generate the resultant faunal assemblages (Grant 1991: 109). As Hill (1996: 18) has noted, a dichotomy exists between the 'ritual' interpretation of human remains
and the 'straightforward' economic treatment of animal bones.

Binford's (1983) work among the Nunamiut of Alaska has
already been referred to, and this provides another key example
of how the economic has been privileged over the religious or
symbolic in this area of study. Part of the focus of this research
was upon the generation of faunal remains, achieved through an
examination of processing activities, centred primarily on caribou.
The distribution of faunal remains is thus considered in various
contexts within the Anavik Springs site complex – butchery
areas, meat storage caches, differential bone-dispersal patterns,
including the so-called 'drop' and 'toss' zones (ibid.: 153) generated

by people processing material while sitting around a fire; data on these is provided but they are not really placed within their possible non-economic frameworks.

The apparent sacred aspect of the caribou hunt among the Nunamiut has already been referred to, and the treatment and conceptualisation of animals themselves after death is in all probability hardly a purely secular activity. Lowenstein (1993) describes how among another Inuit group, the whale hunting Inuit of the Tikigaq peninsula in northern Alaska, existence was related around the sacralising of the earth, and also how the very peninsula itself was considered to be the body of a whale-like creature killed by the primal shamanic harpooner. For our purposes here, practically this meant that when whales were killed, dismembered, and stored underground they were thought of as joining the mythic whale's body.

Lowenstein (ibid.: 33) also refers to the use of whalebone in the construction of *iglus* and *qalqis* (ceremonial houses). These are semi-subterranean structures whose entrance tunnels are built of whale ribs, jaws, vertebrae and scapula – unheated, and thus ambiguous as semi-domesticated places between the world without and the domestic chamber within. Two bowhead jaws were also usually mounted in the walls/ceiling of the inner chamber of the *qalqis*, meaning that the *Umailiks* (whale hunters) 'danced, sang and exchanged gifts within whale jaws that the founding *qalqi* owners had built around them' (ibid.). Furthermore, and although Lowenstein does not make this point, it could be suggested that the use of whalebone as a building material within the earth might also have been of significance, returning perhaps once again to the notion of the sacrality of the whale as the giver of life, and its metaphorical conception as the very land itself. Thus the whale, the primary focus of subsistence activities amongst this Inuit group, has to be considered as much more than the focus of economic logic, and it is highly unlikely that the related Nunamiut are devoid of non-economic conceptualisations surrounding caribou, even if these are completely differently conceived and perhaps expressed to a much lesser degree.

Major textbooks on faunal remains and their analysis similarly neglect the possible religious/ritual dimension. *The Archaeology of Animals* by Simon Davis (1995) for instance, covers themes such as reconstructing past environments, seasonality, or the origins of domesticated animals; religion and ritual, such key features potentially structuring diet and animal use, are almost wholly ignored. Equally, even ideology, animism, anthropomorphism, symbolism and sacrifice, all possible categories associated with animal bone remains are absent in the index, and in the content therein. 'Hunting ability' (ibid.: 152) is suggested, for instance, as a reason for the domestication of the dog, perfectly plausibly, but why not its domestication so as to also be consumed and perhaps killed in sacrifice as well (see Simoons 1994: 200–52)? Why should functional 'logic' predominate as the reason for domestication and the exploitation of animals? Even hunting need not be structured by economic rationale alone, for Ingold (1986: 243) has advanced the hypothesis that the hunt is like a sacrifice, 'a drama often imbued with religious significance, involving some kind of exchange between mankind and the spirit world'.

Yet improvements are evident in the acknowledgement of a ritual (more rarely religious) element in archaeological approaches to faunal remains (see, for example, Anderson and Boyle 1996). For instance, the development of the concept of 'structured deposition' has been a step in the right direction, literally inferring the meaningful deposition of articulated and disarticulated animal remains, human remains, and other deposits (knapping debris, pottery, etc.) within, for example, ditches in neolithic causewayed enclosures, and barrows in southern and eastern England (see Thomas 1988; Edmonds 1999, amongst others). However, it is not without its critics. Bradley (2000: 123) has suggested that ritual can permeate every part of social life and need not be confined to the shrine alone; in other words, the reasoning behind structured deposition is the creation and subsequent focus upon 'special' contexts when a broader overview might be more beneficial. Alternatively, improvements in archaeological approaches to the study of faunal remains are evident in Reitz and Wing's (1999) recent textbook *Zooarchaeology*, which although separating out 'ritual' contexts as temples or burials, at least in contrast to Davis's (1995) volume discussed earlier, recognises that animals can have 'symbolic significance beyond their potential as food, raw material, labour, or exchange' (Reitz and Wing 1999: 274).

Yet this is very much just the start in acknowledging the potential of archaeological consideration of religion/ritual as opposed to, or allied with, an economic rationale structuring diet and animal use. Numerous examples can be found which indicate that economic 'logic' does not necessarily structure animal use and consumption. That of the value of the chicken in West Africa provides a case in point. Of obvious economic significance for both meat and eggs, since its initial introduction in the mid-first millennium AD (MacDonald 1995: 51), it has assumed a primary role in ritual practices in the region. Its sacrificial function, for example, is well attested in the ritual completed at Dafra, the shrine and sacred forest in Burkina Faso described in the Prologue.

MacDonald (ibid.) has attempted to assess why the chicken is so pre-eminent in this respect, when other domesticates such as the dog and guineafowl, similar in terms of value, are readily available. He argues that this was in part due to their 'difference' – they were introduced and 'exotic' (ibid.: 55) rather than indigenous. Equally, MacDonald is at pains to point out that it is the chicken ritual rather than 'alimentary value' (ibid.: 54) which is of greater significance. Hence when an attempt was made to introduce the plumper Rhode Island Red breed in the 1980s into parts of West Africa, though initially a success, it was soon abandoned. The anecdotal reason for this was that when attempts were made to use the new breed for sacrifice in divination rituals its heavier breast meant it kept landing on this, rather than on its side as was desired. Thus the experiment was discontinued and more 'traditional' chickens, though less meaty, were reverted to.

An idea of similar non-economic reasoning, or rather, in this instance, complex reasoning underpinning food use and consumption, can be gained from historical sources as well. Achaya (1994: 61) has examined these issues with regard to the Aryans, the people linked with the *Rigveda*, one of the 'textual roots of

Hindu religious tradition' (Chakrabarti 2001: 35) dating from
*c*. 1500 BCE. Overall, Aryan ideas underpinning food were that
it was 'not simply a means of bodily sustenance; it was part of
a cosmic moral cycle' (Achaya 1994: 61), a cycle in which food
ingested gave rise to three substances, the densest being faeces,
that of intermediate density being transmuted into flesh, and
the finest, *manas*, of 'thought or mind'. Equally, the consumption
of food was structured by complex ritual where every item on the
eating leaf 'had its exact position and ritual eating order' (ibid.:
65). Food was consumed seated on the ground, silent, alone,
facing east or north, with frequent casting of morsels into the fire
for ancestors and gods, with portions of food being reserved for
dogs, Brahmins, serpents, insects and crows, the latter messengers
to the spirit world.

How would this be approached through archaeology? It is
unfortunately elusive, but as archaeologists we have barely even
begun to consider the religious and symbolic factors possibly
underpinning diet – conceptions, components, consumption,
and residue – and their implications for our material. This
stands in contrast to our anthropological colleagues who indicate
the scale of the task which faces archaeology. This is attested, for
instance, by the literature surrounding the debate over the origins
of food taboos, where by way of example the contrast exists
between Mary Douglas's (1966) position as outlined in *Purity
and Danger* on the one hand – that food taboos give religious
adherents a sense of identity and are best understood in the context of spiritual pollution, a premise which in turn, according
to Latham (1987: 389) who provides a convenient summary, has
methodological implications in largely precluding an overview,
as a specifically ordered universe is created for each society –
and that of Claude Lévi-Strauss's ([1964] 1994) more universalistic position on the other hand, specifically as outlined in *The Raw
and the Cooked*, that through analysis of myth the cooking of food
can be seen as a kind of language expressing thoughts and ideas,
manifest in food taboos and structured in binary oppositions.
The whole, again according to Latham (1987: 390), underlain
by the premise that it is 'unnecessary to examine each food

taboo in great detail . . . [as] all cultures will be found to have similar structures'.

Otherwise it is unnecessary, and impossible (but see Latham 1987) to summarise here the relevant literature relating to the development of food taboos, but the important point is that it indicates the differences in methodology and perspective which can exist in relation both to recently extant societies and well-documented historical processes considered within this area of debate, as opposed to the more intractable archaeological data with which we must often deal. Essentially, the recognition of complexity is again the key, the recurring element within the archaeology of religion running through definition, theoretical approach and methodological practice.

Logic has been questioned as a necessary structuring principle for diet; rationality can be similarly doubted. Religion can structure diet, but ideals can remain idealistic, and practice may be pragmatic – as is often indicated archaeologically in regard to Muslim dietary laws for example (see Insoll 1999a: 93–9, forthcoming b). Health equally need not be a major factor surrounding what is consumed or domesticated, but disgust and fear – otherwise seemingly irrational psychological factors – can be (see Simoons 1994). Complexity is certainly there, but perhaps the true key to understanding the possible relationship between diet, animal use and religion, as it also is with studies focused upon death and gender, is to understand that it forms a component of a broader package, and treat it as such, a part within the whole, rather than the end in itself.

## Post-processual approaches

Having considered something of particular aspects of contemporary approaches within the archaeology of religions it is now necessary to broaden out the focus to examine much wider theoretical issues, and how these pertain to our discourse on archaeology and religion.

From the personal perspective of this author a post-processual philosophy, a 'contextual archaeology' (Hodder 1992: 15) or

76

'interpretive archaeology' (Thomas 2000), provides the most useful framework for approaching the complexities of the past, allowing as it does for multiple interpretations, individual agency (see, for example, Dobres and Robb 2000), the active role of material culture, the recognition of past complexity, the use of complex ethnographic analogy, and the realisation that the role of the interpreter is not a neutral one (see Hodder 1982, 1992). However, the positive and inspiring aspects of post-processualism pertain to its general philosophy rather than to its approach to religion in particular, and here it is fair to say that post-processual scholarship has largely neglected religion, even if it is guilty, as Brück (1999: 325) has noted, of stressing the 'symbolic aspects of human action' at the 'expense of the practical'. Ian Hodder, for instance, within the otherwise inspiring *The Present Past*, includes a brief chapter on ritual and though he rightly notes that 'the process of compartmentalisation of archaeology has pushed off ritual' (1982: 159), he serves partly to ensure that this dichotomy survives by emphasising the use of the term 'ritual' throughout rather than that of 'religion', of which ritual usually forms an element. But at least Hodder considers some of the complexities inherent in the label 'ritual', even if religion is not explicitly considered.

It could be asked if the avoidance of using the term 'religion' within post-processual approaches is perhaps in part due to the fact that it is seen as too broad a label, ascribing some sort of similarity in phenomena which allows for no diversity within. Thus Hodder, in considering the 'domestication of Europe', again emphasises the 'symbolic and apparently irrational' (1992: 241) explosion of evidence which occurs, even though some of it might more plausibly be described as 'religious' (also see Hodder 1990). The ritual and symbolic dimensions of material culture are placed within a primarily symbolic framework where, for example, we see the various skulls and boar tusks found set in walls and into clay protuberances at the neolithic site (*c.* 6400–5600 BCE) of Çatal Hüyük in the Konya region of central Turkey (see pp. 81–3) interpreted as functioning to incorporate the dangers of the wild 'within a domestic symbolism' (Hodder 1992: 254).

This might be so, but equally it could be suggested that such an approach does not really engage with the aspect of the intangible, the numinous element of belief which extends beyond a functional conceptual framework. Yet equally Hodder (1990: 11) is completely right in stating that 'the full range of the complex of meanings is lost to us'. This perhaps is the crux of the issue in isolating why religion is avoided in post-processualism in favour of ritual. Precisely for the reason that ritual is concerned, to a greater extent, with action in relation to material things, whereas religion is much more complex – to say what it is, and more importantly what it means, is much more difficult.

The use of the term 'religion' has, it can be further suggested, perhaps been conceptually tainted within post-processual contexts by the sorts of generalising approaches to 'prehistoric religion' previously described. Nonetheless, the absence of religion within post-processual discourse is a glaring omission within a theoretical approach otherwise concerned with recovering the maximum amount of information on all aspects of the past – the 'thick description' of contextual archaeology (Hodder 1992: 245).

Equally, if we as 'archaeologists wander the winding and seemingly endless corridors of post-processual archaeology' as defined by Shanks and Tilley (1992: 7) we find a similar absence of religion. Archaeologists may well be involved in a discourse mediating past and present in a two-way affair, but Shanks and Tilley's construct of the past with its absence of religion within their posited theoretical construct is, to draw upon their definitions once more, really only a reflection of their own 'modernist sense of self-identity acting in and on the world' (ibid.: 251). Ritual might be considered, but religion is subsumed within ideology which is in turn wrongly defined as 'an aspect of relations of inequality' (ibid.: 130). This is not a position which is agreed with here for it is a conveniently simplistic categorisation of religion under a Marxist framework, as discussed earlier, and one which can be further undermined.

For example, ideology is also described as serving 'in the reproduction rather than the transformation of the social order' (ibid.). This is incorrect, the acceptance or imposition of one religious tradition upon another is not necessarily merely 'reproducing' social order, it can fundamentally alter it, literally 'transform' it in many ways, as evidenced by the wave of jihads which swept parts of Western and Central Africa in the eighteenth and nineteenth centuries, the effects of which are, furthermore, archaeologically recognisable (Insoll 2003). For something couched within a post-processual framework it is remarkable how this perspective upon ideology removes individual agency, through somehow suggesting that everyone en masse is hoodwinked or deluded by the false ideology which is religion. Similar criticisms of Shanks and Tilley's approaches to temporality have also been made (Dietler and Herbich 1993: 249), where it has been noted that besides denying the 'non-Western or pre-capitalist the capacity for abstract thought', the complexity of temporality (see p. 129) is also ignored.

The absence of religion within post-processual approaches is a recurrent theme. Julian Thomas (1996), for example, has considered in detail the notion of 'Being' with reference to the work of Martin Heidegger, and rightly indicates that 'human existence is thoroughly embedded in the world' (ibid.: 17). However, 'being' as it is presented is primarily a secular entity, which anthropological material indicates to be a far from universal concept. Among the Yoruba for instance (see pp. 102–6), Thomas's premise about 'being' is shown to be correct: 'the body is the mind' (Drewal and Mason 1997: 333), and it is embedded in the world, but this is also a 'being' immersed and inseparable from religion as well, as the case study considered on pp. 101–19 indicates. It is also apparent that the notion of soul can be locked into that of 'being' as well within certain religious frameworks (Peters 2000: 383). This is something which has as yet to be fully engaged with by archaeologists, and once again we are returned to that irreducible, indefinable element which can also form a part of being – mind, body and soul combined. But this is not to say, in Bell's words (1997: 182), that 'religion defines the nature of human beings, humanness defines the nature of religion'.

As noted, the absence of religion within post-processualism is probably more a reflection of the practitioners of post-processualism themselves rather than any limitations in the evidence they discuss. 'Homo seculariosus' just might not deem religion important and hence it is omitted from their archaeological vocabulary and interpretation. Within a post-processual framework recognition of self and its possible biases upon archaeological interpretation (i.e. the context of the observer) are, rightly, defined as important, being the 'autobiographic experience' (Shanks and Tilley 1992: 251) which brings into existence archaeological experience. Hodder, for example, discusses some of the background which moulded his writing of *The Domestication of Europe*, discussed previously:

> From Camus's *The Outsider*, to the Vietnam war and the events of soixante-huit, from socialism to yuppiedom, from modernism to post-modernism, the issues of structure in relation to change, society in relation to the individual and of science and economy in relation to culture were often at the fore.
>
> (Hodder 1990: 19)

Hodder here isolates modernity as a factor in his autobiographical experience. As with the Enlightenment, the concept of modernity is also of great relevance within an evaluation of archaeology and religion for it too has functioned as a philosophical limiting device for many archaeologists in how they conceive religion. It is characterised by what Thomas (2000: 14) describes as 'metanarratives' such as, 'the rise of the West, the emancipation of the human spirit, universal progress, the development of economies, [and] the growth of democracy'. This would, inevitably, have an impact upon archaeological interpretations of religion, for it involves in essence 'the reification and radical separation of culture, nature, mind, body, society, individuals and artefacts' (Thomas 1996: 29). Religion was thus further abstracted from daily life.

Modernity might rightly be critiqued for its intellectual legacy regarding archaeology and religion, but equally post-modernity offers no solutions either. Post-modernism is defined by Gerholm (1988: 194) as 'a fragmented cultural universe combining elements from various cultural systems', and is characterised according to Johnson (1999: 162) by 'incredulity toward metanarratives' (and see Lyotard 1984). In general terms the relationship between archaeology and post-modernity has been undefined, for, as Whitley (1998: 23) describes, 'it is not yet certain where they will go, beyond an aesthetic and intellectual celebration of multiculturalism'. Hodder (1999: 149) is equally uncertain, describing the post-modern world as containing 'a collapse of perspective, a lack of fixed point except that lack'. Not really a viable starting point for approaching the archaeology of religions either.

But to return to post-processual approaches and religion, perhaps then, many Western archaeologists are from the pool of what Eliade (1978c: 12) has defined as 'the agnostic and atheistic masses of scientifically educated Europeans'. Whereas from the perspective of this author religion(s) are essential, having come from a background of being immersed within them, yet simultaneously studies such as this one are also grounded in different world circumstances to those of even a decade ago, as today religion has (rightly or wrongly defined) become much more of an issue on the world stage than it was previously. Archaeology is again mirroring, as it inevitably will, wider trends (as discussed earlier).

Yet it should also be acknowledged that the role of religion is also increasingly being recognised within recent archaeological research which can be framed within a post-processual philosophy. A good example of this is provided by the renewed work at the aforementioned site of Çatal Hüyük (see, for example, Mellaart 1967; Hodder 1997a, 2000). However, this said, the term 'religion' is rarely used to describe the relevant material here and perhaps the reticence evident is in part a reaction to the original excavator's creation, based upon archaeological data, of a complete religious system for the former inhabitants of the site supposedly centred on a mother goddess type figure (Mellaart 1964, 1967).

But the contemporary rarity of 'religion' as a descriptive device must also be a reflection of the caution being exercised generally in dealing with a site as sensitive as Çatal Hüyük, a site described by Hodder (1997b: 693) as visited by 'bus-loads of people on "Goddess tours"' interested in a spiritual connection with the site, or coming to pray, or connected with Ecofeminist or New Age movements. The multiple roles of Çatal Hüyük as manifest by its function within New Age religion, and its completely different role in Islamic Turkey, has meant that the investigators have had 'to take a stand and not to participate in Goddess events so as not to confront local feelings' (Hodder 2000: 11). Overall the ambivalent status of Çatal Hüyük has further meant that a 'reflexive' approach has been adopted, allowing for 'contextuality, interactivity, multivocality' (Hodder 1997b: 699); in other words, a post-modern perspective.

The adoption of this interpretative perspective has also generated criticisms which in themselves provide an interesting example of the collision of different theoretical worlds, as in Fekri Hassan's (1997: 1021) argument that archaeologists need to stand by 'the methods of science against dogmatism, chauvinism, demagoguery and idiosyncratic beliefs and revelations'. Within the framework of this study, as stated previously, neither belief in the immutability of science nor the confusion of post-modernism provides the solution to the archaeological investigation of religion; a mid-point is again preferable, though an acknowledgement that sensitivity is required is certainly needed.

Mellaart (1964, 1967) was, as noted before, not so reserved in his use of the term 'religion'. He describes religion as constituting 'the community's most important archaeological contribution' (Mellaart 1964: 9). The fantastic preservation at Çatal Hüyük allowed Mellaart's interpretative imagination to be freed. Some 40 shrines and sanctuaries were described as being uncovered, with wall decoration in most, detailing, for instance, a recurrent focus upon images associated with death on eastern walls, vultures attacking headless human bodies being a famous example; or on the Western walls, scenes dealing, conversely, with life, a goddess giving birth perhaps. Burials were also rich. According to

Mellaart (ibid.: 5) the dead were buried inside houses – largely women and children in contracted positions, and stripped of flesh or exposed before final burial wrapped in a cloth, and in association with grave goods which included jewellery with women and children and obsidian arrowheads and flint daggers with men. Numerous figurines were also found, including a 'Holy Family' (ibid.: 10), the Great Goddess with a daughter and young son beside her, with other figurines found denoting a bearded 'god' on a bull, 'perhaps the Great Goddess' husband' (ibid.). A full religious system was proposed, based upon the archaeological evidence.

However, Mellaart's interpretations have been revisited by Lynn Meskell (1998: 47) who makes the point that 'the Catalhöyük discovered almost forty years ago is very different to that being excavated today'. Meskell also critiques Mellaart's emphasis of the 'Great Goddess' as a reflection of the contemporary visions of the 1960s, and hence with the recreation of Çatal Hüyük as presented, 'a utopian refuge for creative, beautiful people to make art and worship the divine female principle' (ibid.: 54). The very presentation of the archaeological evidence by Mellaart in his creation of the Goddess religion is further questioned. The distribution of figurines is criticised for being wrongly interpreted, with most found outside the 'shrines' not inside, whilst Meskell (1998) similarly argues that excarnation was not practised. Moreover, and perhaps most fundamentally, the division made by Mellaart between shrine and non-shrine structures is criticised by Meskell as not being clear and she argues for a blurring of 'the boundaries between what we would call religion and secular' (ibid.: 56) – an insight in agreement with the premise of this book, even if her use of 'we' is something of a general assumption.

It is probably also pertinent to reflect on the fact that Meskell's reinterpretations of aspects of the Çatal Hüyük data are likewise, inevitably, a product of their time as well – and one could suggest that in 20 years, if current fashions persist, the inhabitants of Çatal Hüyük will be interpreted as followers of shamanic practices! Nonetheless, future predictions aside, the advance in techniques over the course of the past 40 years has also, of course, assisted in the presentation of a more detailed picture of religious and ritual practices at Çatal Hüyük. A useful example of just this is provided by Boivin's (2000) recent work on the microstratigraphy at the site, something which is of greater relevance beyond Çatal Hüyük or even the neolithic in Anatolia as she has found a reasonably convincing way of measuring time through archaeological sequences.

This has been achieved through comparing ethnographic data collected in the village of Balathal in Rajasthan, India, with the microstratigraphy composed of multiple plaster layers applied in buildings in Çatal Hüyük. For example, Boivin noted that the yearly cycle in houses in Balathal was represented by the replastering of floors annually, at a major Hindu festival such as Diwali, with a special red soil plaster, known as Laksmi soil 'due to its association with the goddess Laksmi' (ibid.: 370). The individual life cycle was represented by replastering of floors with good quality red soil to coincide with marriage, or also evident in the everyday plaster used for Mausar, the Death Feast, which takes place 12 days after cremation. Based upon these observations, Boivin (ibid.: 380) interpreted a similar rationale underpinning the replastering sequences at Çatal Hüyük, but extended it to include walls as well. Thus thick layers of plaster were considered the residue of annual ritual, and thin layers linked with 'no particular fixed schedule' but perhaps associated with occasional life-cycle rites as needed.

Accordingly, in Boivin's research on a less visible facet of the archaeological data from Çatal Hüyük, we have the type of detailed, convincing interpretation proposed, which although referenced within a ritual framework is what should compose the building blocks of the archaeology of religions – as opposed to the grand sweeping generalisations based on reconstructions of Mother Goddess worship. Yet the application of the term 'religious' need not be an act to be afraid of, even at Çatal Hüyük with all its interpretative exigencies. What the cumulative evidence from Çatal Hüyük indicates, if anything, is that religiosity – of undoubtedly complex and varying forms, thereby rightly eluding characterisation with labels such as 'ancestral' or

84

'Mother Goddess' based – permeated all facets of life. This is also a general realisation that can lock well with a post-processual archaeological philosophy, that, as already stated, religion can be the superstructure into which all other aspects of life are placed, albeit obviously necessitating an evaluation on a case-by-case basis to infer to what degree the archaeology of religion is total.

## *Archaeology, phenomenology, and landscape*

Phenomenology is a further element used within post-processual archaeology which is relevant to our consideration of contemporary approaches to the archaeology of religion. Phenomenology might have been abandoned by historians of religion as an unachievable ideal, as has already been described, but as a theoretical and methodological tool it was utilised relatively recently by archaeologists and thus forms an accepted part of theoretical archaeological approaches within certain circles.

The positive and inspiring aspects of post-processualism were briefly outlined previously, but phenomenology is more problematical primarily for the reasons for which it was abandoned within the history of religions; that is, the inherent limitations of the present upon the contemporary observer in recreating past experience, the 'effort of active empathy' critiqued by Renfrew (1994b: 6). However, it should be noted that phenomenology as applied within archaeology does not make explicit use of the 'principles of understanding' – namely, eidetic vision and *époche*, critiqued previously. Equally, it should also be noted that archaeological phenomenology owes a debt to different philosophical influences than those previously described as influencing the phenomenology of religions. Prominent influences on the former include those of Heidegger (1971) and Merleau-Ponty ([1962] 2003).

The essential premise of phenomenology as applied within archaeology is common sense – it being, according to Tilley (1994: 12), 'about the relationship between Being and Being-in-the-world'. However, with a few exceptions, it can be suggested that much of its application within archaeology has not moved far beyond the starting point of this immediate recognition for the fact that the 'being' in question, basically the modern observer, as described previously, is difficult to project backwards in time. It could be argued that phenomenology stands at the other end of the archaeological extreme from cognitive processualism (see pp. 92–7) in its fundamental antagonism 'to the kind of rationalism whose contemporary manifestation, in the field of psychology, is cognitive science' (Ingold 2000: 168), with this polarity being centred on the notion of the individual as important in phenomenology as opposed to the universal bodies of cognitive processualism.

Intriguingly, the application of phenomenology within archaeology would also seem to mirror the contemporary social currents of Britain, where it was predominantly initially explored – that is, the post-Thatcher legacy of individualism as opposed to society as a whole. It has also been suggested that much phenomenology would be critical of the notion of the individual as a universal trans-historic category, it being recognised that a person is positioned historically, culturally, and through their personal biography, and not necessarily assumed that they have a given and primordial individuality (J. Thomas, pers. comm.). Yet this accepted, it is still the case that within the archaeological study of religion both the individual and society need acknowledging, for religion itself functions at various levels.

The dominant area in which phenomenological approaches have been employed within archaeology is in reconstructing past landscapes, including sacred ones (see, for example, Shaw 1999). Tilley (1994: 9–10) describes its development and application in this area of research as a reaction to processual New Geography, analogous in its theoretical and methodological foundations to those of New Archaeology already described. Phenomenological approaches to landscape perception certainly recognise the complexities inherent in landscape and its role in passing on and encoding 'information about the ancestral past' as a key building block in creating individual consciousness and social identities (ibid.: 40). Ethnography is used to begin to understand something of this function and meaning of landscape, as with Native Australian landscape conceptions centred on the dreamtime creation (see, for example, Myers 1991; Rose 1992).

Yet beyond gaining an appreciation of the possible role of landscape in the past, the difficulties remain in attempting to 'experience' or 'reconstruct' similar meanings for past landscapes. This is difficult enough to achieve for contemporary landscapes through 'outside' eyes − in this instance those of this author. Dafra, the shrine that was described in the Prologue to this book, provides a case in point. It is possible to begin to learn something of the shrine and its embeddedness within the landscape because of supplementary sources (indigenous informants, oral tradition, etc.), but our understanding is only partial and it would be presumptuous to assume otherwise (see, for example, Layton and Ucko (1999) for a discussion of similar issues). Likewise, what is learnt both factually and experientially about Dafra is only really applicable to Dafra, or at best a partial understanding of Bobo perception within this region of Burkina Faso. It cannot be extended directly beyond here, though it certainly can broaden interpretative horizons − what Fowler (2000: 114) has termed in relation to Tilley's work, 'an experiment in modern expression rather than in finding the "truth" about the past'.

Equally, Thomas (2001: 174) has recently argued that diversity of landscape perception means that it would 'be unwise to impose any particular example onto the pre-modern European past', for the precise reason that 'the bodies in recent post-processual landscape archaeologies' (ibid.: 181) are those of modern academics. A cogent point, for in effect what we get in many attempts to 'experience' past landscapes via phenomenology is the suppression of 'culturally patterned thoughts and values' (Davis 2001), which even today are critical factors in determining the variability evident in perceptual skills inherent in coding, viewing and reading landscape. Landscape is thus reduced to 'same', when same does not apply today − does the Amazonian rainforest or a municipal park in Britain mean the same to everyone? Needless to say, it almost certainly did not for the past either.

Tilley (1994: 22), for instance, throws up a somewhat simple dichotomy between capitalist landscapes, a useful 'disciplinary space of social control' and pre-capitalist ones described as also invested with power, 'but within a qualitatively different landscape invested with mythological understandings and ritual knowledges intimately linked with bodily routines and practices'. This would hardly seem to account for the variability possibly inherent in the perception of landscape – the complexities and differences which might even exist within different perceptions of the same landscape. India, for example, constitutes a capitalist landscape, dotted with software houses and factories, but does this mean then that Hinduism is thus stripped of mythic interpretations of landscape so that it slots within the 'capitalist' category? Unfortunately, phenomenology as applied in reconstructing landscape perception sometimes begins to resemble processual Middle Range Theory, albeit couched in post-processual terminology and applied to perceptive rather than cultural material, but similar in the use of ethnography from one part of the world dumped onto the past in another.

To this criticism can be added others. Layton and Ucko (1999: 12–13), note, for example, that 'experience is never adequate to determine which of many possible theories is correct' and that 'expressions of cognition or meaning in the environment are often ambiguous'. Fleming (1999) is also critical of the specific archaeological case studies Tilley uses to apply his phenomenological approach to, indicating that, for example, the heterogeneity of the neolithic tombs examined in Pembrokeshire in south-west Wales 'does not encourage the belief that their designers had a common mind set', and overall that it is 'unconvincing in terms of the archaeological record' (ibid.: 120, 124).

Quite what constitutes a sacred as opposed to a secular landscape is also a complex issue, and one whose definition is also often based on modern perceptions drawn from a limited area of the world. Indeed, the very distinction between the two is not necessarily a useful one for the same landscape can mean different things to different people, and can be one and the same, and thus lack any arbitrary division. This is very much the message of recent work completed on Bodmin Moor in Cornwall: that these 'unwarranted distinctions' (Bender *et al*. 1997: 149) are unnecessary; but still a tendency persists 'to maintain a distinction between sacred or ritual landscapes, and secular or mundane landscapes' (ibid.).

Cooney's (1994: 33) discussion of neolithic landscapes in Ireland for example, though not a phenomenologically inspired one, can be critiqued for making far too simple a distinction between the secular and the sacred, whereby 'what could be defined as a secular landscape is one concerned with everyday life – home, field and farm – while the sacred would be identifiable as containing special places – for example sites for ceremony and ritual, including tombs'. Such a definition is disagreed with here for we have no way of knowing that such a simple distinction was maintained – a definition which furthermore justifies archaeological attention upon 'built' monuments of ritual/religious significance largely divorced from their overall contexts. A dichotomy is established, already extensively criticised herein, between everyday/secular and other/sacred. In equal likelihood such a distinction was not maintained, or at the least the contents of the two categories – secular or sacred – was not fixed in such a manner, but rather could and did vary.

Ethnography, including that within the same volume from which Cooney's paper was drawn, shows the complexity inherent in what can comprise a sacred as opposed to a secular landscape, and the frequent meaninglessness of such a distinction. Ovsyannikov and Terebikhin (1994: 59), in discussing the sacred landscapes of the Nenets in the Arctic region of the former USSR, make the point that for this ethnic group their 'sacrificial sites constituted the "holy book" of the tundra, preserving memories of the people's history and individual destinies'. The whole landscape was interlinked and interwoven in sacred tradition, so that, for example, the southern, male end of a seasonal reindeer migration path was marked with a 'pathway' sanctuary, Kozmin Copse, a place also marking calendrical change and the seasonal transition from reindeer husbandry to hunting (ibid.: 72). Hence here the potential indivisibility of sacred and economic (secular) landscape is well indicated. Equally, it also signals, in effect, that what constitutes a sacred space can defeat

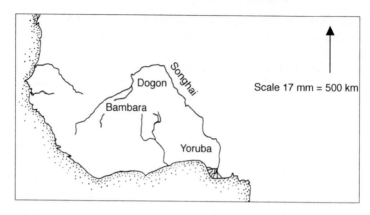

*Figure 4* Map of West Africa indicating locations of principal ethnic groups
mentioned

the categorisation of the archaeologist, perhaps schooled in the
'built' cathedral or mosque; instead it can be a tree, a wood, or
a whole landscape, or many other things (see Chapter 4). Once
again the past can be 'other' – our categories of the sacred are
not uniform, and we need to expand our interpretative horizons
in order to encompass the available possibilities within the archaeology of religion through drawing upon supplementary sources
such as ethnography.

A further useful example of the power of ethnography with
regard to exploring our categorisations – not for direct comparisons in recreating 'experience', but as a source of ideas on
how the sacred and secular are hard to divide in the landscape –
is provided by Zahan's (1974) study of the Bambara of Mali
(Figure 4). Among the Bambara the landscape would appear to
be of great significance in interlocking within various spheres of
life, and must be imbued with different degrees of knowledge
and belief depending upon who was viewing it. These could
range from the initiated member of the *komo* brotherhood,
through to the more generally accessible domains of knowledge
surrounding the many features which are scattered across the landscape, both natural and human-made. The placing of sacrifice

stones by crossroads, besides the River Niger, or in fields, or the citing of ritual pots covered with small mounds of earth also in fields, pots which are watered to encourage the earth to remain damp and thus the millet to grow (ibid.: 32), are examples of the latter. However, trees such as the *sunzu*, 'the tree of proliferation' (ibid.: 8) or the kapok tree, the symbol of the soul (the appropriacy of this term is unclear), mind and subtlety, are also key elements of the religious landscape, as can be features such as springs or rocks, perhaps through acting within the *dasiri* cult, itself relating to 'attachment' or 'fixation' and thus focused upon the foundation points of settlements.

Within the Bambara landscape the interweaving of both natural places and features created by human action renders an explicit division between what constitutes the sacred and secular difficult. But equally, perception of this landscape would also seem to vary. It would appear to be by no means uniform, but instead based upon degree of knowledge and place in society, and, it can be suggested, individual interest in such issues, often forgotten, is surely an important factor as well. Complexity would again seem to be an appropriate key word here.

In general and in summary, perhaps a more profitable approach to adopt within the archaeological study of religions, in respect of landscapes, is the type of holistic perspective employed by Richard Bradley (2000) in including the 'unaltered places' within his overall archaeology of natural landscapes. Or indeed, in terms of more nuanced theoretical approaches to the notion of 'being', i.e. to phenomenology, the more critical reflexive perspective employed by Thomas (1996, 2001) which is aware of the inherent limitations. Yet, as noted earlier, there can be major problems in the archaeological application of phenomenological methodology. Too frequently it is glibly applied, as if it offers an insight into past experience denied through more conventional archaeological techniques. Obviously this is not the case; a phenomenological understanding of death, for example, regardless of the more idealistic perspectives of some archaeologists, will prove permanently elusive – one tries, one dies. Certain mysteries will remain, mysteries which underlie much of the archaeology of religions.

## Cognitive processualism

Previously it was described how processual approaches within archaeology had largely neglected religion as a principally un-investigatable domain. Yet more recently, chiefly but not wholly due to the early impetus of Colin Renfrew (1985, 1994a), 'cognitive' processualism has developed within which the archaeological study of religion has a definite place. This is defined as differing from the 1960s positivism which characterised the New Archaeology in that it lacks the 'singular critical tests favoured by processualists', having developed a more 'sophisticated' methodology, while at the same time being linked to its parent processualism in arguing from the theoretical perspective that there is still 'a true and objective past' (Pearson 2002: 22). This is a development from Renfrew's earlier more strictly processual approaches whereby a 'framework of inference' was called for 'which would allow one to make warranted statements about the past, in this case about past cult practice and religious belief, on the basis of archaeological evidence' (1985: 11). Again, to draw on Pearson (2002: 33) who supports a standpoint of truth and objectivity, cognitive processual archaeologists 'conceive the past as existing in the physical world (much like the present), with human beings living their lives and interacting with each other and their environment very much as we do today'; in other words, the universal 'we' which was referred to in Chapter 1.

Yet fundamentally, cognitive processual approaches to the archaeological study of religion (and indeed, to the past in general) suffer from the same problems as their parent processualism: the assumption of 'same' between past and present, the essential human condition across time and space as a given (the generic 'we' in the quotation just cited), the existence of rules or guidelines which somehow structure past belief and action, and the suppression of the individual. Post-processual individual 'empathy' might be criticised, but equally the cognitive processual attempt to enter the mind – a collective mind – is equally unachievable. Renfrew's 'Mappa' is flawed, the internalised cognitive map 'which we believe to be part of the shared human condition' (1994b: 10). The essential hard-wiring of the human condition might be there but the assumption that 'we' are all basically the same today as in the past is not necessarily viable; it reduces the past to 'same'.

Within the perspective of this volume, the appearance of anatomically modern humans might be correlated with the gradual appearance of religion, or at least a predilection for such, but as has already been noted it is not assumed that commonalities exist in terms of interpretative insight in so far as this author is an anatomically modern human and so can fully understand the early modern human communities of perhaps 90,000 years ago (see Chapter 1). No, the presumption in itself is flawed, we cannot be certain that our cognitive insights based on contemporary observation are the same as those of the past. Otherwise we reduce everything down to an essentialist outlook, defined by Johnson (1999: 87) as 'the belief that there are certain attitudes or emotions . . . that are "natural" or biologically endowed, either to humans in general or to a specific sex'. This is inherent in psychological approaches to religion, as exemplified by Pascal Boyer's (2001: 318) statement that he sets out to describe 'religion in terms of cognitive processes that are common to all human brains, part and parcel of how a normal mind functions'.

Yet such a perspective underscores the work of David Lewis-Williams (2002), for example, and although he is not uncritical of aspects of cognitive processualism, the supposed cross-temporal notion of 'rational intelligence' (ibid.: 111) for instance, he too assumes an essentialist standpoint. In his work in interpreting the meaning of upper palaeolithic rock art within a shamanistic framework he draws upon the writings of the historian of science and philosopher Giambattista Vico and his concept that 'there must be a universal "language of the mind" common to all communities' (ibid.: 51). But does cultural weight invalidate such generalities? The hard-wired structural principle of the human condition might be correct, but the differential weighting of culture, even if only manifest in multiple subtle nuances placed on different elements within, leads to infinite variety, in turn weakening the notion of a universal 'language of the mind'.

This too is leaving aside the analogical jump which is being made from the ethnography used to enrich the shamanistic interpretation of the upper palaeolithic rock art – ethnography which is drawn, primarily from the San people of southern Africa, and has been used to ascribe a similar three-stage trance or altered state of consciousness model as recorded amongst the San upon the motifs depicted in European caves. This has been much criticised (Solomon 1997, 2000; Kehoe 2000; Bahn 2001; Helvenston and Bahn 2002) and need not be repeated here; it is not the focus of our attention, though in the end it could be noted that such an interpretation would not appear to be particularly new. For instance, Hawkes (1954: 162), writing in the early 1950s, mentions and condemns as a 'very long shot' the use of direct analogy 'from the side of the modern South African Bushmen and the significance of their paintings, back to prehistoric Africa, and then maybe European, Stone Age paintings'.

Similarly, Lewis-Williams also provides a perspective on the Enlightenment, derided for promoting reason, 'allied to positivism, intolerance and fascism', but continuing that 'there is no getting away from the conclusion that the Enlightenment opened up the possibility of knowing that the "voices" came from within the human mind, not from powerful beings external to it' (Lewis-Williams 2002: 288). But for many the voices are external, they defy rationality and the universalistic assumption that they should fit within a presumed logically derived source. That is part of the complexity of the archaeology of religions which remains unacknowledged in cognitive processual approaches.

Shamanism would also appear to be a recurring favourite target of cognitive processual attention, reinforcing the dichotomy in approaches which often occurs according to which specific period is being investigated. Thus a gulf seems to exist between the neolithic and the palaeolithic in terms of approaches to religion and ritual, with, for instance, phenomenology rarely applied in the latter and cognitive processualism likewise largely absent in approaching the former – in other words, prior philosophical 'territories' are somewhat unhelpfully demarcated. Thus Winkelman's (2002) study of shamanism is linked with cognitive evolution, again with a universalising emphasis evident whereby 'the neuropsychological basis of shamanism is manifested in cross-cultural similarities in shamans' characteristics' (ibid.: 72). Hence Winkelman further posits that shamanistic elements were already part of cultural practices in the middle palaeolithic, and that cave-art images represent shamanic activities and altered states of consciousness. But in the end, the same problems of positivism, universalism, assumption and analogy render such cognitive processual models too inflexible in what they attempt to incorporate within them, even taking into account the claims made as to supporting 'neurognostic structures' (ibid.: 73) and psychological data.

Nash (1997: 57) might also attempt to overcome some of these hurdles in invoking a Jungian psychoanalytic approach as a way of getting at landscape meaning, including the 'surreal or fantastic quality'; in the end, though, the same assumption of similarity to that just described weakens his study. The 'archetypes' or 'prime imprinters' described as 'inherent in human nature' (ibid.: 58) can be suggested as merely psychological equivalents supposedly generated by the unconscious mind of the material 'Hierophanies' or 'axis mundi', the notion of recurring spiritual centres developed by Eliade (1959). Nash is assuming, and indeed states, that perceptions of landscape, including features frequently defined as 'ritual' or 'religious' in nature, remain the same across time, owing to the assumption that 'the psyche (conscious or unconscious mind) of the fully modern humans of 40,000 years ago was not significantly different to that of people today' (1997: 58). This search for the 'collective meanings' is essentialist in outlook and reductionist in scope. Continuity might be there but the existence of unconscious archetypal similarities on an enduring scale raises the inevitable question of whose collective archetypes are being invoked. As already stated, the assumption of similarity is not proven.

Likewise, the role of analogy is stressed within this study (see Chapter 4), a major element within cognitive processual methodology, but this is advocated here within a less binding manner: as a tool that can expand our interpretative horizons, if anything in making us aware how different the past might have been 'other', but not as something to provide direct parallels (see pp. 113–16). Finally, to reduce religion within the cognitive domain to something that can be somehow mapped is also in error, for it does not take account of that element already introduced, the irreducible 'numinous' component of religion, which although it cannot be assumed that it is universal and means the same thing for all humans – societies and individuals – is a factor which has to be considered. If one considers much religious data what is in fact apparent is chaos, variability, uncertainty and diversity as expressed in religion itself, religious practice, religious affiliation, and, one assumes, by inference the accompanying mindsets as well – the very target of the cognitive processualist's attention.

Renfrew (1994a: 47) recognises the problem of carrying 'to the inquiry our own culturally-encapsulated, and therefore perhaps stereotyped, view of what religion is', but then seemingly proceeds to ignore this to a certain extent as for example in his discussion of the recognition of 'cult' (Renfrew 1985). The problems with the term 'cult' have already been described and, within the approach to the archaeology of religion espoused within this book, religion as influencing all categories of life and hence material culture is argued for; but this does not mean checklists exist. Whereas Renfrew (1994a: 51), though arguing that a 'mechanical check list' is inappropriate, then proceeds to provide one, so that we get 16 'archaeological indicators of ritual' grouped within four categories:

- Focusing of attention.
- Boundary zone between this world and the next.
- Presence of the deity.
- Participation and offering.

The embeddedness of religion might be recognised, but practically its archaeology is once again separated out into a 'cult' niche, as ultimately explained by the point that it is 'only where religious practices involve either the use of special artefacts or special places, or both, that we can hope to discern them archaeologically' (Renfrew 1994b: 51). Cognitive archaeological approaches are weakened by the fact that religion is separated out and placed in a definable box, as for example within Flannery and Marcus's (1998: 47) discussion as to why cognitive archaeology should not form a separate branch of archaeology – hence religion, as one of the 'products of the ancient mind', is placed alongside cosmology, ideology and iconography. The mind is certainly the key, but religion can be the framework defining the other elements just described, rather than sitting alongside them.

## Indigenous religions and contemporary issues

The realisation that archaeology can be of immeasurable use in furthering our understanding of indigenous religions, especially those of non-literate peoples (i.e. in contexts where other sources of evidence might be lacking), is also a direction of contemporary research. This has led to re-evaluation by some archaeologists that 'what makes something sacred to people of a different culture may have none of the characteristics or trappings of those things or places they consider sacred in their own society' (Hubert 1994: 11).

This has proved to be especially the case where ethical issues and indigenous peoples are involved, as with these issues surrounding access to and protection of Native American sacred sites. The whole question of what defines a sacred site has had to be considered by archaeologists, and great compromises made by Native American religious leaders in asserting 'themselves publicly, to reveal information previously kept secret' (Bean 1992: 3). Theodoratus and LaPena (1994: 21), for instance, describe how for the Wintu of northern California topography was considered essential for the maintenance of their cultural identity and continuity, and how great loss was felt when significant locales were destroyed, changed, or had access to them restricted through, for example, the construction of 'non-Indian' developments such as railways, roads, and habitation areas, allied with factors such as mining and deforestation.

One way to begin to address such problems is to include an indigenous perspective within relevant archaeological projects. This is exactly what the Kohla Project in the Annapurna Himal region of west-central Nepal has attempted (Evans 1999; Pettigrew and Tamu 1999). Thus the project aim to 'search for a more authentic version of the past' (Pettigrew and Tamu 1999: 329) was addressed by including shamans within the project team. This was undertaken both as a way of beginning to unlock the meaning of landscape through integrating the *pye*, the sacred oral traditions of the Tamu shamans which include within them lists of places passed through when the Tamu migrated into Nepal, seemingly from Mongolia, but also as a way of negotiating access both to specific sites and the landscape as a whole. Hence just the sort of issues alluded to previously within the North American context were avoided through negotiating via the shamans with the ancestors and gods of the area, specifically according to the shaman Yarjung, 'to let them know that we respected them and to ask their permission to do our research in their area'.

Evans (1999) and Pettigrew and Tamu (1999) are forthright in describing the results of this collaborative venture. In general the list of places contained in the *pye* seemed to agree with what was recorded on the ground, as they note that 'landscape corroborates the shamanic version of the past' (Pettigrew and Tamu 1999: 340). But differences between archaeological and shamanic interpretation were also evident. For example, a variety of marks recorded upon a large rock were interpreted as signs of 'ritual activity' by the archaeologists, to the amusement of the indigenous people who said these were marks made with sickles while people rested, smoked and chatted.

In the Kohla Project the inclusion of shamans and an indigenous perspective brought a new dimension to interpretation, but this is something frequently undertaken in a less overt manner by many other projects. Where the importance for our purposes lies here is in the aspect of negotiation as well as in the interpretative outcomes. The acknowledgement of indigenous sensitivities within the archaeological study of religion is vital and is very much a growing element, rightly, of contemporary theoretical perspectives and methodological approaches.

But collision could and can occur where some sort of religious 'common ground' is perhaps assumed, as has happened in certain instances between neo-shamans and indigenous communities. Neo-shamanism is defined by Wallis (2001: 213) as 'a spiritual path among Westerners that utilises aspects of indigenous shamanism and representations of shamanism in the past, for personal and communal spiritual empowerment'. However, Norton (1992: 228–31) highlights how a collision between the individual 'egoic needs' (ibid.: 228) of the neo-shaman can come into conflict with the more communally focused activities of traditional shamans, within, in the particular circumstances he discusses, North America. This is perhaps a reflection of what Bowie (2000: 197) describes in the wider context as the individualistic and universalising tendencies of neo-shamanism, which she argues is 'very much in tune with much of what is loosely described as New Age religion'.

Thus not all instances of relations between researchers and indigenous communities are necessarily as amicable and productive as those enjoyed by the Kohla Project. A further related example is provided by the so-called reburial issue in the USA, and the allied Native American Graves Protection and Repatriation Act (NAGPRA) which was brought into effect in 1990 (see, for example, Watkins 2000; Swidler *et al.* 1997; Fagan 1998). This legislation was implemented as a result of strong objections voiced about the display of Native American human remains and also to 'the mass warehousing of hundreds of thousands of Indian skeletons' (White Deer 1998: 333) within the USA. As White Deer comments (ibid.: 334), similar practices were not carried out with regard to other groups in American society, but the indigenous population were thought of as somehow the exception. NAGPRA thus affects four types of Native American cultural items held in museums – sacred objects, funerary objects, human remains, and the broader category of 'objects of cultural patrimony' (Watkins 2000: 56).

Prior to 1980 consultation with indigenous groups as to what archaeological research was being pursued was not even deemed necessary, leading to a situation, according to Watkins (ibid.: 21), whereby 'American Indians tend to equate archaeologists with pot hunters, grave looters, or, even worse, animals who feast off the dead'. Although there is much debate over the effectiveness of NAGPRA, and the associated National Museum of the American Indian Act which was brought into effect in 1989 (ibid.: 16), it does illustrate that contemporary approaches within the archaeological study of religion are, in certain instances, beginning to encompass the notion that much of the material studied can be of active significance to groups not previously considered.

# 4

# THE CASE STUDIES

## The archaeology of traditional religions and Islam in West Africa

The three case studies which have been included focus upon dimensions of the archaeology of traditional religions and Islam in West Africa. They have been chosen as they allow a consideration of past and contemporary approaches to the archaeological study of religion in West Africa, and also an evaluation of various critical elements of much greater general relevance, both methodological and theoretical, which need to be included within an evaluation of archaeology and religion. Thus three examples will be integrated: first, a focus upon Yoruba religion, and in turn the role of analogy and the place of emotion; second, an outline of Dogon religion (see Figure 4, p. 90), which also allows an examination of the potential of myth as an aid to research; and, finally, a brief consideration of the relationship between Islam and traditional religions, allied with an assessment of the concepts of 'collision', time and syncretism, the latter being a term referring to the processes of religious blending or fusion which can occur.

### *Yoruba religion: analogy and emotion*

Yoruba religion functions as a useful case study for our purposes in a number of ways. First, it introduces a relevant body of material not often known outside of African archaeological circles. Second, it indicates how elusive convincing religious categorisation can be; third, it allows us to draw together a number of strands touched upon only in passing thus far: the role of myth (itself considered in greater detail in the Dogon case study, pp. 119–23) and the potentially all-pervading nature of religion. It also permits the introduction of the concept of emotion as a powerful force in religion, and thus in the archaeology associated with it – for here emotion is directly indicated in the archaeological evidence. Furthermore, the potential of this Yoruba case study as a source of analogy for broadening interpretative horizons, in approaching what could be termed 'otherness', can also be evaluated.

## *The Yoruba: category and definition*

The Yoruba are an ethnic group who in 1993 numbered some 30 million people found predominantly in south-western Nigeria, Togo and Benin (Olupona 1993: 240–1) (see Figure 4, p. 90). Within the types of religious classification systems already described (and critiqued) in Chapter 1, Yoruba religious practice would be characterised as 'traditional', thereby providing an example of African traditional religions. However, scratch below the surface and again the inappropriacy of these simplistic divisions is exposed, not least in the fact that Yoruba religion, or rather aspects thereof, forms part of religious systems participated in by several million more people in the New World.

Examples of these include Candomble in Brazil and Voudou in Haiti. The former has been described as a 'collective African memory on Brazilian soil' (Ortiz 1997: 90; and see Bastide 1978), in which Yoruba elements include the presence of the deity Ogum or Ogun (discussed further on pp. 118–19). Voudou, likewise, has been described as 'essentially Dahomean' (Métraux 1989: 29) in origin, a reference to a former kingdom to the west of Yorubaland in the modern Republic of Benin in West Africa, though it also has Yoruba elements. This is because, as Hurbon (1995: 15) relates, in the eighteenth century the Dahomean royal family in the city of Abomey sought to extend its power by appropriating deities belonging to its enemies such as the Yoruba. Yoruba religion, along with many other African beliefs, was in turn spread to Haiti, and throughout other parts of the New World by the Atlantic slave trade operating from the West African coast between the sixteenth and mid-nineteenth centuries. Yet the process has not stopped there, for Barnes (1997b: xv) also discusses how such religious traditions have subsequently been further spread by Brazilian and Caribbean emigrants to the United States, Canada, and Europe. Thus Yoruba religion has, to adapt another point made by Barnes (1997a: 1), a 'meta-cultural' aspect to it as well, which means, for instance, that it eludes a single language or ethnic group ascription, described as defining recognition criteria in the checklist for traditional or primal religions in Chapter 1.

In addition, Yoruba religion is also elusive in attempting to define what it actually is: monotheistic, polytheistic, animistic, ancestral. It defies categorisation in being composed of multiple elements, having a supreme god, Olódùmarè, remote but the focus of people's ultimate devotion. Equally, there are many lesser gods who are also the focus of devotion, as can be the ancestors, but the latter are not the focus in themselves but one of several avenues of connection with the supreme god (Awolalu 1979). Spirits of earth, lagoons, rivers, the sea, wind, trees, hills and mountains are all found as well, but, as Awolalu (ibid.: 49) notes, 'it would be wrong to call the whole religion animism'. This in itself, it can be suggested, carries warnings for our categorisations of past religious systems which were probably similarly conceived as more flexible, complex and ambivalent than our neat reconstructions of neolithic ancestor 'cults' or mesolithic shamans allow.

The ways to the gods are likewise multiple and complex. Yoruba religion can be seen to function at both the level of the individual and the community, and the access points to religiosity reflect this. Prayer can be personal, as individual circumstances, desires and outcomes dictate, but it can also occur in a communal situation. Similarly, song, dance and masquerade function at a communal level, whilst sacrifice can function at both levels, communal and individual (Awolalu 1979). The primary purpose of the latter ensuring, according to Adediran and Arifalo (1992: 313), 'the continuous benevolence of the deities'. Here again we can suggest that comparable complexity underpinned much of past religious systems as well, complex manifestations in how devotions were offered, devotions which functioned at a variety of levels both individual and communal.

We can also likewise explore this dimension of Yoruba religious practice through archaeology, and the focus here will primarily be upon archaeological research completed in the city of Ife, regarded as the spiritual epicentre of the Yoruba. A city where archaeology has indicated that by the fifth century CE the scattered villages in the area around Ife began to fuse into multi-village polities, and where between the tenth and eleventh centuries formal kingship and urbanism appeared. This period prior to the twelfth century is designated the Pre-Classic, and was succeeded between the twelfth and sixteenth centuries by the Classic period. The latter is described as the focus of most archaeological research by Ogundiran (2002: 41), and characterised by the production of naturalistic bronze, brass and terracotta sculptures, by the delimitation of urban areas with walls, and by the laying of potsherd pavements (see Garlake 1978). The Classic was in turn replaced by the unsurprisingly termed Post-Classic of the sixteenth to nineteenth centuries (ibid.). Our emphasis is upon the Classic period, and besides being the focus of the majority of the archaeological research completed, it should also be noted that this research has largely in turn focused upon shrines and burials. This might be convenient for our purposes, but overall, limits our understanding of the totality of Yoruba life and belief through archaeology, so recourse is also made here to oral tradition and ethnography.

Equally, a definitional problem arises which should also be noted. This is that many of the structures investigated have been referred to as 'shrines', which in itself provides a further instance of the inappropriacy of available classificatory terminology. The reason being because 'shrine' is derived ultimately from the Latin *scrinium* – meaning 'box' or 'receptacle', as in 'containers of sacred meaning and power' (Courtright 1987: 299), and it can thus be suggested is a term which singularly fails to describe the range of structures included within its boundaries. It is this notion of boundaries which is vital, for in creating 'shrines' we again define boundaries, bounded space, which might not in reality be so easy to demarcate as we might desire. Again, as with religious categories themselves (see pp. 139–45), neat boxes do not necessarily exist. Our assumption of definition is just that, assumption, as can be seen when Yoruba 'shrines' are considered.

In contemporary terms these 'shrines' can include both prominent and hidden structures, prominence conceivably being attested by placement at a crossroads, or conversely hidden away and known only to the initiated (Awolalu 1979: 115). The 'shrine' could also comprise a built structure (Figure 5), traditionally marked by being surrounded by a thick bush or situated in a grove marked by trees such as the Peregun (*Dracoena fragrans*) or Akokoa (*Newbouldisa leavis*) tree (Adediran and Arifalo 1992:

*Figure 5* Shrine in the Ore Grove, Ife (copyright Frank Willett)

313). Alternatively, it could be a tree itself, the silk cotton or iroko perhaps; or a hole in the ground offered libations; or likewise a pile of stones similarly treated (Awolalu 1979). In this instance, the latter structures are better referred to as altars rather than 'shrines', as indeed they are by Awolalu (ibid.). Other scholars, however, could be less cautious in their definitional ascription and thus what are patently altars might become 'shrines' as well, again indicating the definitional clarity which 'shrine' lacks. Nonetheless, alternatives are hard to find, and thus 'shrine' is a term which will be used here, albeit allowing for ascriptional subtlety between shrines and altars when required.

But the material dimension in itself is not the be all and end all of the shrine or altar; the human element is vital as well. Drewal (1997: 241), for instance, describes how the Ogun altar is established with two or more pieces of iron, sacrifices, 'and the voiced prayers of humans'. Sound is critical – sound generated by prayer, as here, but also the dimensions of rhythm, song or chant. Equally, smell can also be crucial. Drewal and Mason (1997: 335) also relate how the power of the masker (Egungun) who represented a lineage's ancestral warriors at Abeokuta in Nigeria resided in the power packets sewn onto his clothing, the words of praise which energised these, the kinetic energy of the crowd and accompanying dancers, and also the 'pervasive over-powering stench that emanated from its blood-soaked tunic'. Prayer, and potentially the sounds of sacrificial victims, drum-ming, song, the smell of blood, sweat and faeces are all divested from our archaeological material, but all could have helped consti-tute our elusive 'other'.

## The archaeology of Ife

This would certainly appear to have been the case with some of the archaeological material from Ife, as with that from Peter Garlake's (1974) excavation of a Classic period site, Obalara's Land. This was composed of several stone and potsherd pavements which seem to have been courtyards within domestic buildings, with various groups of objects outside these buildings 'purposefully arranged in a way that suggests they were offerings at a shrine' (ibid.: 111). However, this somewhat prosaic description belies the complexity of the material recovered. For example, within one of these pavements (B), formed of chunks of quartz and ironstone set within areas of potsherds, a pot had been embedded as its intentional focus, indicated by four concentric circles of sherds and stones laid around it (ibid.: 117). This pot had on its shoulder eight carefully modelled reliefs depicting:

- A rectangular structure like a box with a cloth or palm frond fringe, and inside three terracotta heads: a central one with overall scarification and a complex headdress, at right a simple cone with stylised eyes and mouth, and at left a similarly stylised head but with the top formed of three projections or knobs.
- A pair of human legs and feet depicted from the thighs down projecting from a basket, interpreted as a sacrificial representation.
- A pair of conical objects joined on a cord suspended from a peg, and interpreted as *edan ogboni*, ritual symbols of the Ogboni cult.
- A skin-covered drum similar to the Yoruba *igbin* drum.
- A knife for slashing rather than piercing.
- A flail or short whip.
- Diametrically opposite the pair of conical objects a pair of animal horns joined by a cord and suspended from a peg.
- A possible torque or manilla.

A snake rendered in naturalistic style curves around the vessel above the reliefs with its head reaching down to the centre of the roof of the shrine containing the three sculptured heads. That this vessel was a libation vessel was suggested to Garlake (ibid.: 143) by it having had its base removed prior to being inset in the pavement, hence offerings could be poured directly into the earth, and overall it is interpreted as being linked with Ogboni, the 'Earth God' (ibid.: 145). This posited link is further strengthened by the depicted *edan ogboni* already described, as well as by the representation of sacrifice. The presence of sacrificial imagery is not confined to this single pot either as it was also found on another vessel from Obalara's Land depicting gagged and decapitated human heads, itself similar in turn to a vessel from Ita Yemoo, also in Ife, which had reliefs depicting a naked, bound, decapitated corpse and a gagged decapitated head (ibid.: 130; and see Willett 1959, 1970).

On its own the pot just referred to is obviously not necessarily indicative of the types of dimension just described as potentially energising religion, but it was not a solitary occurrence. Other material found at Obalara's Land included sorted piles of human remains, such as a compact group of complete and fragmentary human skulls comprising eight complete crania (minus mandibles), 14 complete calvaria, eight almost complete calvaria and fragments of a further five calvaria. Their condition would seem to indicate that they were collected together some time after decapitation or post-mortem. The uppermost skull had resting against it a terracotta head depicting 'an expression of malevolence or horror' (Garlake 1974: 122). Another terracotta head of a diseased individual was placed close by, along with further terracotta and pottery fragments, and human long bones. Garlake (ibid.: 146) suggests that the human remains are not 'the direct result of execution or sacrifice' but are rather of people who died of disease whose heads were disposed of separately as a preventative measure so that the disease did not recur. Alternatively, Ogundiran (2002: 50–1) has suggested that ritual decapitation was carried out on people of different social classes in Ife, within an overall ritual practice involving 'post-mortem human decapitation, multiple burial ceremonies for the elite, human sacrifice, the sequencing of offering ceremonies at specific altars and shrines, and the use of terracotta and copper-alloy sculptures to service burial ceremonies'.

This concentration of material was found south of a feature interpreted as having been a timber structure, itself represented by an area 2 metres in diameter almost devoid of finds other than large numbers of iron nails. North of this putative timber structure, a possible 'shrine', was another concentration of artefacts,

comprising pieces of terracotta sculpture including six torso fragments and four naturalistic human heads, as well as two stylised
ones. In contrast to the two terracotta heads found in association
with the skulls, which were modelled with close cropped hair and
as unscarified, and depicted 'emotional and realistic representations of misery and horror' (Garlake 1974: 144), some of these
other terracotta heads were decorated with intentional scars.
These included both facial and head scars and, on one female
figurine, body scars from the waist to beneath the breasts and
arms (ibid.: 131). Colour was frequently used on these figurines:
white for scars and red for skin.

In summary, Garlake (ibid.: 144) suggests that this latter group
of terracotta heads were predominantly rendered as idealised and
unemotional, relics with 'immanent and intrinsic power' and
treated with reverence even if damaged. Stretching away from
these terracotta fragments for a distance of some 3 metres 'was a
mass of human long bones' (ibid.: 123), with two iron rods, and
a decorated iron staff resting on top of these, the latter described
as reminiscent of the *Opa orere* or *osun* of Yoruba diviners. At the
end of this pile of long bones nearest the terracotta heads, the
bones had been covered with a dense concentration of potsherds.

The evidence just described, though unique, is representative of
other finds both within Ife and its wider region, with the same
emphasis upon structured deposition, post-mortem treatment of
the dead and sacrifice. Ogundiran (2002: 47), for instance,
describes a thirteenth-century burial from Iloyi, 50 km north of
Ife, as containing a decapitated skeleton in association with a
variety of material, including two grinding stones; two quartz
slabs; jar and bowl fragments, some containing dry and burnt resi-
dues possibly of food; a skull of a sheep/goat and fragments of a
land snail shell. Eyo (1974) excavated a shrine dated to the early
twelfth century at Lafogido Street in Ife containing a group of
inward-facing terracotta heads accompanied by a group of pots
capped with figurative lids set in a rectangular arrangement.

The site of Ita Yemoo has also been referred to. Here, among
a mass of material recovered (Figure 6), Willett (1959: 135–7)
excavated two bronze mace heads in a group of other objects

*Figure 6* Figurine fragments emerging during the excavations at Ita Yemoo
(copyright Frank Willett)

interpreted as originally placed in pots upon the potsherd pavement of a royal shrine (the latter ascription indicated by the bronze figure of an *Oni* or king of Ife found there). The larger of the mace heads depicted two human heads, one with a plump face gagged with a twisted rope, the other of a wizened elderly man also gagged. Similar gagged heads were depicted upon a bronze staff head; the function of these objects was interpreted by Willett (ibid.: 137) as used for symbolic blows before the sacrifice or 'for stunning or even killing the victim'.

Historical and ethnographic sources also describe various ways in which the dead have been treated prior to burial, and although treatment differs, they indicate that the archaeological material from Ife was not anomalous. Examples include the practice of drying the corpse by a fire for later burial, recorded among the Ijebu Yoruba, or the preservation of parts of the body for secondary rites as in the kingdom of Benin which neighboured Yorubaland, and where hair and nail parings encased in chalk served as a substitute for the corpse (Poynor 1987–8: 81). The latter, by way

110

of an aside, suggesting all sorts of interpretive possibilities for the depictions of soft body parts such as phalli, found modelled in chalk or clay at various sites from various periods, as with, for example, certain sites dating from the neolithic in England (see, for example, Smith 1965).

## *Emotion*

In general, what we can take away from this brief and highly selective consideration of the evidence, primarily from Ife, is the awareness that what we are dealing with is far from sterile. The emotional and sensory facets of smell, noise, terror and exhilaration, identified as present in contemporary Yoruba religion through ethnography, would all have been palpable in creating this archaeological material. Yet much of what we read and write about as archaeologists is seemingly posited on a logical, reasonable and comfortable foundation; rationality as discussed earlier predominantly formulates our intellectual horizons. However, it could be argued that some of the material we encounter as archaeologists was underpinned by alternative perspectives beyond those of our everyday experience. The past could truly be other, and again ethnographic analogy can assist us in exploring 'other' dimensions which might inform our archaeological interpretations. For example, the emotions of horror, fear and terror are not necessarily absent from religion; they are not all generated by divine beauty and good, and an element of such emotions must have underpinned aspects of the Yoruba material just described.

Moreover, complexity again has to be recognised, for emotions and actions can be placed in alternative and conflicting frameworks to those which might be rationally expected. Hall (1997: 32), for example, recounts how among the Native American group the Huron, the torture and killing of captives would frequently be framed within a perspective of adoption and even love; how victims would be adopted by someone who had lost a son in war. Parents were then given the job of 'caressing' (torturing) the victim, as, for instance, in couching the application of a hot iron in the form of a necklace as a way of making the captive

111

beautiful, and therefore it being undoubtedly something they would love to endure. This does not mean that we shall ever encounter such a scenario archaeologically, nor is it particularly related to religion, but it does indicate the complexities involved in the conceptualisation of emotion which can exist. Emotion, though 'hard-wired', is not necessarily always conceptualised in the same way. Reaction to pain, for example, can differ significantly; everyone feels pain, but the way it is dealt with can vary according to cultural context, as with reactions to childbirth and susceptibility to torture for example. Indeed, as Merleau-Ponty ([1962] 2003: 219–20) has discussed, 'the psychophysiological equipment leaves a great variety of possibilities open'.

This notion of the complexities inherent in emotion, and their potential for archaeologists, though not within the framework of religion, has recently been considered by Tarlow who makes the point that although the 'capacity for what we might call 'emotional' experience' (2000: 716) is universal, the emotions themselves are not necessarily universal. This is crucial for our purposes for religion is linked with emotion. It might be controlled or displayed above and beyond that of normal life in certain religious contexts, but it is often there in the background embedded within and intertwined with religious thought. The numinous, as described earlier, is in essence irreducible from emotion, and, this accepted, emotion is thus critical as a generative factor in the archaeological material we consider.

Yet the potential of an archaeology of emotion as a sub-discipline is rightly acknowledged as a path to nowhere by Tarlow (ibid.: 729). Rather, it can be suggested that emotion forms but another element of the complex of factors of which we should be aware within the archaeological study of religion. The recognition of emotion should also be separated from that of the role of the senses – sight, sound, touch, taste – within the archaeology of religions, as something more profound, the deeper result of sensual stimuli. (See, for example, Houston and Taube (2000) for a consideration of the archaeological recovery of sensual perception, as retrieved through an evaluation of iconography in Meso-america – though here it could be argued that some of the material

considered is in fact inseparable from emotion.) The acknowledgement of an emotional factor in the archaeological study of religion
also returns us back to where we began in this section in that it
further reinforces the place of ethnography as a wonderful resource
in indicating the possibilities of the 'otherness' of the past, including that pertaining to emotion.

## Analogy

Furthermore, with such superb evidence as that described from Ife
it is also tempting to let one's imagination loose in scooping great
dollops of ethnography as interpretative glue for the archaeological data. For example, the contemporary use of white fluid
squeezed from snails to soothe cuts made by body artists (Drewal
1997: 244) could allow the exploration of potential links between
snails and scars, and in turn the associations between terracotta
scarred heads and the deposition of snail shell fragments. However, restraint shall be exercised here, tempting as the runaway
train of analogy might be, for close as the links seem between
Yoruba ethnography and the archaeology of Ife and its region,
several centuries separate the two.

Equally tempting would be to project Yoruba ethnography
onto some of the instances of structured deposition and secondary
burial found in European prehistory. A case in point is provided
by Isbister, a neolithic chambered tomb on South Ronaldsay in
the Orkney Isles (Scotland) dating from *c.* 5000 years ago
(Hedges [1984] 2000). This was a tomb estimated to have been
built and used over several generations which contained various
resorted remains: 'little piles containing a skull and other bones
along the sides of the main chamber, skulls in the side cells and
residual bones under, and perhaps on, the shelves of the end
stalls' (ibid.: 133). Besides the human remains, various animal
remains were also found in the tomb. These included up to
twenty sea eagles laid in various contexts. The sea eagle bones
formed 90 per cent of the overall total of 97 per cent of bird remains
found which, interestingly, were all of carrion-eating species (ibid.:
145); thus only 3 per cent of non-carrion-consuming species were

present. Other animal species represented in the tomb included cattle, sheep, goats, pigs and red deer, mainly young animals, and hundreds of fish. Also found was carbonised grain, and broken and burnt pottery sherds, as well as bone pins, flints and other stone tools.

This material has been extensively interpreted: by Hedges (ibid.: 139, 157) within an 'ancestral' framework, with the sea eagle seen as a possible 'totem' of identity, and more recently, for example, by Andy Jones (1998: 319) who is critical of Hedges and instead places his interpretation within the framework of an understanding of place built upon 'a wider late Neolithic understanding of the world, which fused the memories and identities associated with place, with the manipulation and deposition of a set of materials which included some species of animals'. These are both worthy interpretations, notwithstanding the aforementioned 'proliferation' of ancestors. One could also certainly draw obvious parallels between the Isbister and Ife material and then use Yoruba ethnography for further interpretative purposes, if one was so inclined. For example, based upon the Yoruba material, it could be suggested that what is evident at Isbister is but one element of a larger and more complex religious package. This in turn could have been focused upon a higher deity or deities, with the 'totemic' or 'ancestral' elements being just that, a part of the religion rather than the religion itself.

But is this really the role of ethnographic analogy? Within the discussion of cognitive processual approaches made earlier, the role of analogy was briefly touched upon and it is now necessary to consider this in a little more detail. The definitions and uses of analogy have been much debated and there is no need to repeat them here (see, for example, Binford 1967; Gould 1980; Hodder 1982: 11–27; Wylie 1985; Oestigaard 2000b: 2–3). Yet the crucial point is that analogy should not be used in the sense of searching for direct parallels between Yoruba religion and Orcadian neolithic tombs, or even 'piecemeal comparisons' which result in archaeologists losing sight, as Bradley notes (2000: 30), 'of the specific evidence they are trying to interpret'. Formal analogies, i.e. that sorted human remains are found in both instances and thus further parallels must exist, are flawed for obvious reasons. Equally, relational analogies – defined by Hodder (1982: 19) as demonstrating 'that similarities between past and present sites are relevant to the "unknowns" that are being interpreted, whereas the differences that can be observed do not really matter; they are not really relevant because there is little link between what is different and what is suggested as being the same' – are not necessarily that useful either as a general category of analogy to be uniformly applied for interpreting the archaeology of religion.

The true potential of analogy is as an aid to the interpretative imagination, and this is a point succinctly made by Oestigaard (2000b: 3) in noting that 'neither anthropological nor archaeological theories based on ethnographic data will totally correspond to a particular prehistoric society, but they might give a fruitful approach to interpretations that may corroborate with the archaeological material'. Within the archaeology of religion, analogy can literally broaden the mind and expand the horizons of interpretative possibility. In the words of Michel Foucault ([1970] 2002: 24), 'it makes possible the marvellous confrontation of resemblances across space; but it also speaks, like the former, of adjacencies, of bonds and joints'.

With regard to the particular example just described, rather than seeking direct parallels, the Yoruba ethnography can again serve to indicate the complexity which almost certainly existed and which might have underpinned the deposition of the material in Isbister; its power exists in again raising the potential of acknowledging the past dimensions of stench, fear, noise, emotion and variability of religious form. It also can be used to suggest that the past processes which created the deposits in Isbister were probably a lot more complex than our posited reconstructions of ancestral creation or late neolithic sense of place and world-view might allow for. Yet we also have to recognise that this is complexity which will remain elusive, but at least we might begin to appreciate the potential of just how elusive and 'other' it might have been, and how the probable 'rich text' which is required is not best served by much of the 'mono' interpretation offered at present, largely predicated upon a rational world-view loaded with a lot of unquestioned assumptions, as already critiqued, and in all probability completely alien to past agents.

### Religion? A return to definition

To reinforce this point it is also necessary to return to the Yoruba once more, and again a question can be framed as to how might we begin to gain a fuller insight into the potential meaning of material such as that recovered from Ife if the direct transference of ethnography is unwise? The answer is to place it in its wider context; that is, as part of an indivisible picture of life whereby religion is not necessarily separated out from everything else. Garlake (1974: 143) might acknowledge that courtyards such as those found at Obalara's Land served both ritual and domestic purposes, but in doing so it could be suggested that he inadvertently promotes division between the two domains where none might have existed. Ogundiran (2002) predominantly approaches burial alone and as such privileges explicit 'religious' or 'ritual' facets of evidence in the manner already described.

Perhaps in beginning to gain a more complete understanding of this material it is preferable to look, obviously, to all facets of the archaeological record, but also at the potential accompanying sources of evidence – not just ethnography, but also oral tradition and myth. Here, a key source of evidence would be the Ikedu Texts, traditions which relate the origins of the people of Ife. These provide a means of starting to get at the 'proto-Yoruba'; but almost immediately a problem regarding this source of evidence emerges which must be recognised. First, they are mythic and religious in 'flavour' (Olaniyan and Akinjogbin 1992: 39); second, it is apparent that only fragments of these traditions are available, for the uninitiated cannot collect them and the initiated cannot reveal them. A conundrum well described by Olaniyan and Akinjogbin (ibid.: 39), overall in relation to Ife, is that it is the place where the 'tap-roots' of Yoruba society exist, and 'tap-roots are not exposed if the tree is to survive'. Hence the realisation must be acknowledged that rather than necessarily gaining specific information from traditions such as the Ikedu Texts, a general impression of factors such as the embeddedness of religiosity can be sought.

In this respect a key insight is that religion can permeate all areas of life, and therefore the type of division criticised previously is flawed. But a crucial question has to be asked here as to whether this is religion as it might generally be defined (as in Chapter 1), or is it just life, devoid of such a distinction or descriptor? This issue can be explored with reference to the concept of Oduduwa, described by Awolalu (1979: 25) as 'a controversial figure in Yoruba belief', who seems to have been an individual associated in Yoruba tradition with initiating and implementing numerous changes. Hence he is linked with the development of Ife as a town, the implementation of the dynastic tradition, the development of bronze casting, the growth in importance of the meaning of beads, the initiator of the concept of the palace and the administration of the state (Adediran 1992), and, it seems, responsible for the formalisation of aspects of Yoruba religious tradition.

Now many of these points could perhaps be questioned on the basis of archaeological evidence: the growth of urbanism possibly. Even the historical person of Oduduwa is unspecific, being described by Obayemi (1992: 62) as 'several co-existing but overlapping definitions of the name, personality, concept or phenomenon called Oduduwa'. Yet this is not crucial for our purposes for we do not seek the historical Oduduwa. Rather, the importance of the concept lies in Oduduwa serving as an obvious metaphor for the start of the Classic period, but also in the full growth of Yoruba religion as influencing and indivisible from all elements of life. Hence previous to Oduduwa we might have knowledge from the Ikedu Texts that there was a supreme being and numerous lesser deities, and that 'some of them presumably deified men and women with physical features such as rivers and rocks' (Olomola 1992: 59), as well as awareness of the fact that the practice of Ifa divination was already in place (ibid.). However, subsequently everything appears to come together in a holistic package whereby we can trace chains of meaning running from religion through many other aspects of life, negating its arbitrary division into a separate defined sphere. Of course, such links might have existed previously in the Pre-Classic period; we do not know (but the initiated might). However, the Oduduwa tradition allows us to be more precise about this in the Classic period.

Technology, for instance, slots into this framework, the functional and non-functional being inextricably intertwined. Iron-working would predate Oduduwa or the Classic period in Ife, but its importance within a ritual or religious framework becomes increasingly manifest. As in the iron staffs described previously from Obalara's Land, or in a pear-shaped hundredweight of iron which serves as the shrine (altar?) of Ogunladin, the blacksmith of Oduduwa, in the ruler's palace at Ife mentioned by Horton (1992: 133). Complex chains of meaning are created between iron and Ogun, and between Ogun in his role as circumcisor, scarifier, carver, excisor and body decoration for example. Thus Olóòlà, the body artist, 'is an extension and manifestation of Ogun' (Drewal 1997: 255) in various ways, through placing individuals by means of their scars in the larger 'social and cosmic universe' in the same way that Ogun creates order by transforming, by means of iron tools, 'the forest into farms and cities' (ibid.). Ogun links can also be further extended into the domain of colour symbolism; he is linked with red and white, the extremes through which iron goes in being created from ore. Moreover, Ogun is fiery; he is cooled, as noted, by snail fluid, but also through the sacrifice of dogs, the dog being a carnivorous animal, 'thus Ogun receives what he is' (Pemberton 1997: 130).

Thus in the end we have returned to ethnography, and the possibilities for exploring the archaeological material from sites such as Obalara's Land with this type of information are all too obvious. Similar chains of meaning could be explored but this is not our purpose here. Rather the important point to note is that the application of a multi-source approach, moving beyond ethnography alone where such sources of evidence are available (and obviously this is not always so), allows the notion of religiosity, its extent, and again the seeming inappropriacy of our definitions to be explored. Furthermore, it can be suggested that the Yoruba example is far from unique. Religion is complex; religion by its nature is shifting; and religion defies ascribed boundaries as in many elements of this 'traditional' religion suiting 'world' religion categorisation or supposed associated complexity. Archaeology provided a key to examining aspects of practice, but archaeology was made more powerful through oral tradition, myth and ethnography – which ultimately served to indicate past complexity, how the past can be 'other', and how elusive past meanings inevitably are.

Finally, bearing in mind the points just made, it should also be noted that the examples chosen do not mean that West African religions are a 'primitive other', but they provide another perspective of experience to draw upon without simultaneously drawing value judgements. Their discussion is not an attempt to create the 'ideologies of otherness' rightly critiqued by Mudimbe (1988: 6–23, cited in Shaw 1990: 342). Equally, the reference to 'experience' does not mean that one can just slot into West African religions like putting on an empathetic glove, but they do provide a body of experience, both collective and individual, which can be drawn upon but not 'lived' from outside the relevant cultural context. The presumption of 'living' or 'experiencing' contemporary Yoruba religious life is not entertained here, though conversely, and again illustrating its flaws, some would presume that just such an experience is possible for communities who existed thousands of years ago. Rather, such data as that just described can expand, to repeat our interpretative horizons when attempting to understand the complexities of past religions, and in so doing reinforces the frailties of our discipline

## Dogon religion: the power of myth

### The laughter of Ogotemmeli?

As was just noted with regard to Yoruba religion, myth provides a further category of evidence which can be used by archaeologists in investigating religion, and both the power and pitfalls of myth as a potential source of evidence can also be considered here with reference to another case study drawn from West Africa.

The Dogon are a people who occupy the Bandiagara Cliffs in Mali, the sandstone plateau at its summit, and the sandy Seno plain at its base (see Figure 4, p. 90). They have been studied since the beginning of the twentieth century by anthropologists, most notably Marcel Griaule (1965), and increasingly by archae-ologists (see, for example, Bedaux 1972, 1991). Dogon religion is complex, and is summarised by Van Beek (1988). The head of the Dogon triumvirate is Ama or Amma, the Sky God, the others being Nomo, the Water God, and Lewe or Lebe, the Earth God. Sacrifices and rituals are primarily directed toward Ama, though carved figurines are also produced by the Dogon, which are 'repre-sentations of the living' (ibid.: 60). However, these too serve as mediators with Ama – in helping to solve problems for instance. Divination is also a key feature of Dogon religion, as are masked dances.

Dogon myth was initially revealed to Marcel Griaule (1965) by a Dogon elder, Ogotemmeli, and subsequently, following Griaule's death, further Dogon myth and knowledge was collected by his colleague Germaine Dieterlen (Griaule and Dieterlen 1965). The essence of these myths is recounted, for example, by De Heusch (1985: 156–9) who describes them as dominated by an 'agricultural code', being a 'mythology devised by and for farmers. God created the world in the form of a minute seed animated by vibrations, and the sacrifice of a "water god" proceeded to permit its bursting forth' (ibid.: 159). The fundamentals of Dogon myth as revealed to Griaule and his successors can be seen almost as an interpretative chain running through and underpinning much subsequent scholarship on the Dogon, with myth being seen as the primary structuring agent of Dogon thought, belief, and also, for our purposes, material culture and world-view. In fact, to quote Clifford (1983: 123), Griaule saw Dogon culture as a 'kind of lived mythology'.

Hence the countryside is described as being 'organized as far as possible in accordance with the principle that the world developed in the form of a spiral' (Griaule and Dieterlen 1998: 94), meaning that, theoretically, the central point of development is formed by three ritual fields themselves assigned to the three mythical ancestors. The village is described as laid out either in a square like the first plot of land cultivated by humans, or in an oval with an opening at one end and thus symbolic of the 'world egg broken open by the swelling of the germinating cells' (ibid.: 96). Villages should also be built in pairs, linked in turn with concepts of 'twinness'. Regardless of the oval or square village plan just described, a body analogy also simultaneously underlies the village form for it is also conceived of as a person lying north–south, with the smithy the head, shrines the feet, family houses the chest, and menstrual huts the hands. Whilst the house itself represents, 'a man lying on his right hand side and procreating' (ibid.: 97), his penis materially manifest as the entry via a narrow passage leading into the workroom in which the water jars and grinding stones are kept (Figure 7). The agricultural essence of the myth could also be further interpreted here in the metaphorical status of the liquid by-products of corn-crushing being seen as analogous with semen (ibid.) – a liquid which is in turn poured on the ancestral shrine.

In other words, almost the whole package of Dogon material culture conceptualisation has been linked with myth. But the mythic penetration goes further for it served, in Griaule's view, according to Van Beek (1991: 140), 'as a blueprint for all facets of society, from the way to cultivate a field and build a house to weaving, pottery making, drumming, and smithing'. Yet these mythic cultural foundations have been reconsidered, as the subtitle to this section implies. The key criticism which has been made of Griaule's interpretation and presentation of Dogon myth is that the picture as presented through his conversations with Ogotemmeli has 'proved impossible to replicate in the field, even as the shadowy remnant of a largely forgotten past' (ibid.: 139). Griaule's very methodology in collecting his data seems to have been flawed, consisting of short visits and paying informants, with the whole overlain by a confrontational style. In the

*Figure 7* Exterior of Dogon hunter's house, Songo, Mali (photo T. Insoll)

view of Van Beek (ibid.: 157), who has reconsidered Griaule's fieldwork, it is 'the product of a complex interaction between a strong-willed researcher, a colonial situation, an intelligent and creative body of informants, and a culture with a courtesy bias and a strong tendency to incorporate foreign elements' (see also Clifford 1983: 124). The net result being that instead, again according to Van Beek (1991: 148):

- The Dogon know no 'proper creation myth'.
- The supernatural Dogon world is more diverse and vague than that proposed by Griaule.

- The symbolism of Dogon religion is more restricted and fragmented – meaning that 'body symbolism is not the basis of house plans or of the layout of fields or villages'.
- Religion in Dogon society is not all-pervasive.

However, it should be noted that Van Beek's (1991) deconstruction of Dogon myth and religiosity, as presented by Griaule, is far from universally accepted, as the comments which accompany his paper which has been drawn upon in this discussion indicate. Certainly an earlier paper by Clifford (1983) is less critical, but in Van Beek's defence it would seem that he has completed the 'detailed restudy of the Dogon' which Clifford (ibid.: 124) saw as a hurdle to the evaluation of the specific criticisms of Griaule's fieldwork. This said, Van Beek's work is obviously also influenced by his own views on religion, acknowledged or unacknowledged, and will undoubtedly be itself re-evaluated, if indeed it has not already been. However, the key for our purposes here is not this, but rather how myth seems to have permeated most scholarship on the Dogon, which in turn can apparently be traced back to the presumption by Marcel Griaule that all would be revealed to him by Ogotemmeli; that *la parole Claire* – 'the highest most complete stage of initiatory knowledge' (Clifford 1983: 146) – was there for him. In so doing, he seems to have believed what could be termed his own myth – a full mythic framework which was subsequently swallowed by numerous other scholars. Myth is useful, myth can be a vital source of evidence within the archaeological study of religion, but myth need not form the basis from which everything else is generated.

## Myth: definition and application

Although a 'cautionary tale' surrounding the application of myth might just have been provided, drawn upon cautiously myth can in fact be of great use. For 'a myth – like a ritual – simultaneously imposes an order, accounts for the origin and nature of that order, and shapes people's dispositions to experience that order in the world around them' (Bell 1997: 21). Yet myth viewed from within a rational perspective is often seen as 'a fanciful tale as opposed to true, discursive language' (Paden 1994: 70), and often confused, as Paden (ibid.: 72) also notes, with folktales, a different form largely concerned with a 'make-believe realm'. This is a useful distinction and one which will be applied here, for we do not want our archaeological interpretations informed by folk or fairy tales, though myth, as it is ostensibly concerned with past reality or perceptions thereof, can be a powerful tool if used carefully and critically. As Claude Lévi-Strauss (1978: 65) has noted, myths are not 'prelogical', it is just that the logic therein might differ from that of Western thinking, itself 'dominated by too narrow a logic'.

Alternatively, and equally unfortunately, myth has often been considered as some sort of raw historical essence – hence in all probability the wariness by archaeologists in using it as a source of evidence. Mircea Eliade, for example, believed that there was an irreducible sacred dimension to human experience which was manifest in myth, particularly in pre-literate societies. Two kinds of time were proposed by him: historical time ('a time that kills') and mythical time ('a time which saves') (Horia 1969: 387–8). This is unadulterated idealism and is not the purpose of myth; it is a harking back to a pure source of the untouched 'peasant', the *La France Profond* of Central Europe. As a universal generalisation such a conception of mythical versus historical time does not work, precisely for the reason, as Saliba (1976: 161) notes, that Eliade and the overall methodology of history of religions, as regards myth, 'does not take seriously into account human social relations, or the cultural background, or the historical context'.

Oral tradition, which is history, and myth are here confused as one and the same, and both critical analysis and definition of source are lost. Scales and frameworks of time are denied by such a concept of myth, but time is of course present in pre-literate societies as much as in literate ones. Myth and oral tradition are not somehow reflections of an embryonic pre-temporal state – the potential pitfalls have already been illustrated with regard to this. Examples are myriad indicating the existence of time frameworks before literacy or the integration of societies within historical frameworks within oral tradition/myth – the proto-Songhai of the Niger Bend in Mali before Islam for instance (Insoll 1996).

Here, the inclusion of ancestors from the Yemen within origin myths reflects the overall Islamisation and Arabisation of history recorded in written chronicles such as the Tarikh al-Sudan (Es-Sa'di 1900). Yet to think of it solely in such a way would be restrictive, for it also reflects the conflation of Islamic ancestors with pre-Islamic time. In fact it is the coming together of various sources, various historical frameworks, and in tandem their associated temporal mechanisms. These include the mythical primordial time of Faran Maka Bote, the first ancestor, through to the time frameworks represented by the four groups which Jean Rouch (1953: 196–9) suggests formed the Songhai: the Sorko, or fishermen; the Do, or 'masters of the water'; the Gow, or hunters; and Berbers, perhaps Christian and perhaps from southern Libya. Hence, it can be suggested that the different ancestral traditions and temporal conceptions enjoyed by these groups, allied with Islamic time-frames, are all present, strands which potentially could be further teased apart and in so doing enhance archaeological interpretation – but only if oral and written sources, myth and history are considered together.

Related to this question of time as recoverable from oral tradition, including oral traditions of mythic character, is the degree of flexibility which is indicated in pre-literate oral societies as regards ritual and religious change. Frequently these are taken to be ascribed fixed structures, with change occurring slowly if at all. Yet such concepts of ritual and religious change are based in the main upon literate societies, where, as Bell (1997: 204) notes, 'change itself easily becomes a problem that is viewed as a threat to tradition and authority'. Flexibility would certainly seem to be the key with regard to the Yoruba example just discussed, and the contrasting lack of flexibility inherent in textually based ritual can also be indicated, albeit with a fictional example. Mervyn Peake's *Titus Groan* (1978) illustrates this perfectly. Lord Groan, under the instruction of Sourdust, has to participate in meaningless ritual after ritual in Castle Groan because that is how they are recorded in the 'great tomes' (see, for example, ibid.: 63–7).

Unfortunately such models derived from literate societies (albeit not from Mervyn Peake's creation!) are then extended outwards to many other societies, frequently inappropriately. This too has fundamental implications for archaeology, and archaeologists once again need to consider their own position when attempting to reconstruct ritual or religious change, for argument's sake in the European neolithic, coming as they do from 'textual' backgrounds. It is also useful to acknowledge that myth and/or oral tradition need not contain essential unchanging structures, but rather, in contrast, can function as a reservoir of ideas on change and adaptation.

Within archaeology the utilisation of myth as a source of evidence in understanding religion is comparatively rare, perhaps because the term 'archaeomythology', like 'archaeoastronomy', has fringe connotations. As already described, these types of sub-disciplinary terms are not particularly useful, but myth itself as an aid to informing interpretation can be in certain instances. An interesting use of myth is provided by Antanaitis's (1998) study of the meaning of symbolism in the eastern Baltic neolithic (*c.* 6500–3500 BP) within which an attempt is made to interpret items such as animal teeth pendants of elk, boar, deer and dog, as well as figurative art including elk/moose-headed batons, and images of water fowl carved on wooden spoon and ladle handles in the light of Finno-Ugrian and Lithuanian myth.

How successfully this is achieved depends upon the definition of success. We learn that the waterfowl 'is among the most recurrent of the mythological motifs of Finno-Ugrians in Northern Eurasia in general' (ibid.: 63), but obviously a direct leap cannot be made to saying that this is what these particular objects meant. A suggestion is there but no more, and in practical reality the use of myth for the purposes of archaeological interpretation is not as promising as scholars such as Eliade might have argued, but it does supplement other sources of data such as the ethnography Zvelebil (1997) uses to interpret a similar body of material. In this instance, Zvelebil draws upon ethnographic case studies, such as the Kets of Podkamennaya Tunguzka of western Siberia as a reference point to begin to reconstruct, for example, mesolithic cosmology and religion as manifest in the cemetery at Olenii Ostrov in Karelia. Sculpted artefacts such as elk-headed terminals are interpreted through analogy as 'shaman's *turu*, a ritual rod used to mediate between the natural and supernatural worlds' (ibid.: 42). Zvelebil is more direct in his use of analogy, and thus feels compelled to defend his position accordingly, but though making reference to myth – the *Kalevala*, 'the Finnish national epos' (ibid.: 45) is mentioned for instance – he does not draw upon mythic or epic material to the same extent as Antanaitis; he prioritises his source material differently.

Prioritisation of source material is a matter of personal preference, but contextualisation of myth is vital. Although Lévi-Strauss was ultimately flawed in seeking what could be almost described as a universal language or structure of myth, his point (1978: 65) that myths should never be interpreted alone but with reference to, for example, 'the ethnography of the societies in which they originate' is common sense. Equally, it could be added, that they should be observed, where possible, within the context of their surroundings as well. Griaule's Dogon myths might have been better evaluated if considered with reference to those of neighbouring groups such as the Bambara, Fulani or Songhai for instance. Griaule might have moved, as Clifford (1983: 123) describes, from 'parts to wholes, to more inclusive wholes', and argued for three regional sub-Saharan African epistemological regions, but the overall comparative framework could have been better rooted; perhaps this failing is also in part a consequence of his 'panoptical aspirations' (ibid.: 135). In this respect the question can also be posed as to where the dividing line between ethnography and myth can be placed; did Griaule lose track of this? We learn about one (myth) frequently whilst pursuing the other (ethnography) or vice versa. For example, Malinowski describes myths associated with the Kula of the Trobriand Islands as 'a fount of ethnographic information' on subjects such as canoe-making and sailing (Strenski 1992: 25).

To return once again to the original focus of this case study, the Dogon. It should also be noted that besides collecting myth, Griaule's (1965) research also provides ethnographic information, and the one blurs with the other. This work has already been described, but its relationship with, and influence upon archaeology completed in Dogon country has not yet been considered. Primarily this is because it has had little effect, perhaps owing in part to the narrow focus of archaeologists working in this region, being still preoccupied with chronologies, for example, as opposed to the deeper meanings of material culture (see Insoll 2003 for a summary), this having saved them from falling into the same traps as some anthropologists as regards the all-pervasiveness, or not, of myth. Equally, it can be suggested that the effectiveness of myth also needs to be measured within the paradigm of who generates it. Within the Dogon example, as described, this seems to have been primarily from an external perspective; indigenous academic 'referencing' points seem to have been absent. In the initial Yoruba case study considered, myth was also integrated, that surrounding Oduduwa for instance, but here indigenous perspectives, those of archaeologists, historians, and anthropologists, served as a cross-check (albeit tempered by the initiated versus uninitiated conundrum), allied with the fact that myth was included as a supplementary source of evidence rather than it being given undue primacy as some form of foundational strata.

## African Islam and traditional religion: 'collision', time and syncretism

The third example to be considered from West Africa allows an examination of world religion, in this instance Islam, its interplay with African traditional religions, and the syncretism which can occur, and how this might be evaluated archaeologically. But more than this, it can also be integrated with the previous examples, as time is of course related to myth and oral tradition, and this case study also allows a brief consideration of time.

## Time

Archaeologists, though concerned through the very nature of their discipline in recovering time and time-related events, are in fact remarkably naïve when it comes to conceptualising and theorising temporality – certainly as regards religion and time. Shelves full of material may exist on the practical study of skeletal remains, or the archaeology of death, for example, but time is still an under-researched subject in many areas of archaeology (but see Bailey 1983; Bradley 1991; Zvelebil 1997; Murray 1999). Miranda Green (1998: 190) might make the point that time 'as a powerful, often sacred, force has long been recognised by archaeologists and anthropologists', a point which in archaeological contexts could apply to parts of European prehistory but little else (excluding archaeoastronomy, which has its own attendant problems and debates – see, for example, Burl (1997) and Ruggles (1998). The archaeology of world religions provides an instance of just such neglect (Insoll 2001a), where time has been ignored and is often treated as a given, with temporal frameworks, if considered, conceived of as identical to those of today, whereby linearity predominates.

However, within religions, both 'world' and others (and hence their associated archaeology), time is vital, for most religions are explicitly concerned with time, controlled, for instance, through the ritual cycle (Bell 1997). Ritual might provide the means to 'recapitulate the past in the present' (Ricoeur 1985: 17), but we should not think of time and associated ritual as eternal, unchanging, fossilised even, for timescales within a religious framework are complex and variable. Various scales of time exist, the so-called 'multilayered' (ibid.) phenomena of temporality which can include both cyclical and linear time as well as time manifest in life events, seasons, fleeting moments of prayer or reflection, the ordered time of ritual, feasts, festivals, and pilgrimage or the disordered time of grief and emotion.

Religious temporal frameworks could assume a significance which goes beyond practical reality. The hypothetical case of practising the Ramadan fast above the Arctic Circle in the extremes of a Polar winter or summer provides a case in point (R. MacLean, pers. comm.). Here, conceivably, one of the Five Pillars of Islam developed in the very different temporal landscape of the Arabian Peninsula could become unworkable, tied as it is to cycles of night and day, and thus must become, if one is to observe it, an internal framework of time, not physically tied to sun or moon. Ramadan is obviously embedded within and generated by the Islamic calendar, in itself a complex system which is based on a lunar cycle of 12 months alternating 30 and 29 days each with a year reckoned to have 354 days, though the last month, Dhu-al-Hijjah, can have an intercalated day bringing the total to 355 days and thus it is normally 10 days shorter than the Gregorian calendar year. Within this a solar reckoning system is used to calculate the start and end of the Ramadan daily fast, while the lunar one is used to determine the month of fasting (Walshe and Warrier 1997: 15). Complexity is the key here, and this is related to a single religion – in itself hinting that past temporal complexities in all their assumed variability were much more so.

A further useful example of complexity which can be introduced at this juncture is that of Australian Aboriginal concepts of time, as manifest in the 'Dreaming'. This is best described as cyclical – 'Dreamings all exist all the time' through their being a 'sea of endurance, on the edges of which are the sands of ordinary time' (Rose 1992: 205). 'Ordinary time' is described by Rose (ibid.), at least as conceived amongst the Yarralin people, the focus of her study, as a period of about a century containing changes which do not endure. In contrast the Dreaming, 'denies creative significance to history and human action, just as it denies the erosions of time' (Myers 1991: 52).

Yet this is not merely a philosophical construct, for the Dreaming is rooted within the types of material which we as archaeologists have to consider. In landscape perception, which is connected through the Dreaming with the ancestors but which is not necessarily completely atemporal, again drawing on the Yarralin, Rose (1992: 206) mentions how 'there is sequence defined by movement through real geographical space'. This is manifest in Dreamings travelling from east to west, but also temporally linked with disjunctions: 'salt water covered the earth before it pulled back into oceans; Dreamings walked in the shape of humans before they became fixed with respect to place, size, and shape' (ibid.).

Time here is cyclical, enduring, and could almost be defined as 'real' in opposition to ordinary time which lacks depth. Thus it could be asked if in imposing our profane, ordered, sequential temporal chronologies to material potentially related to communities who might perceive, partly, of time in a very different way, are we in fact denying complexity and in so doing stripping the past of its riches? Obviously this is an easy question to pose, though no solution is offered here as to how it might actually be approachable; but the notion of time as potentially very complex needs acknowledgement.

## *Syncretism and 'collision'*

Equally, syncretism, the blending or fusing of different religious traditions or elements, can emerge as a practical mechanism for reconciling time. Although sometimes condemned as a contentious term implying 'inauthenticity' or 'contamination' (Shaw and Stewart 1994: 1), 'syncretism' is preferable to alternatives such as 'creolized', and as such will be used here in considering religion. The need for syncretic process to reconcile time can take many forms: time as manifest in an agriculturally aligned seasonal system confronted by and having to integrate a very different system for example. This is precisely what can occur with conversion to Islam when there is of course the imposition of a new calendar, 'arranged, without intercalation, to be independent not only of the old Arabian lunar year but especially of all solar reckoning which was traditionally linked to the structures of agricultural society and religion' (Denny 1985: 71). If agriculture is really a 'ritual revealed by the gods or culture heroes' (Eliade 1959: 96), then the abandonment of associated seasonal, temporal, and ancestral frameworks will be difficult; alternatively adjustments might be made to allow the continuation of old and new combined.

This would appear to be what occurred with conversion to Islam in the Sahel region of West Africa where it is possible to suggest a model of phased conversion allied with syncretic adaptation based in part on archaeological data (Insoll 1996, 2000). Within this region the earliest converts to Islam would seem to have been the nomadic populations, precipitated in part through their early exposure to Muslims by acting as their guides in trans-Saharan trade. But equally, the ease with which they converted is not solely explained by notions of familiarity but also, perhaps, through the degree of upheaval involved in nomadic conversion being less pronounced than that suffered by agriculturalists for instance (see, for example, Levtzion 1986). Hence factors such as the ease of worship which Islam enjoys would have been significant, allied with the potential lesser importance ascribed to physical ties to the land, and in turn to the degree of ancestral significance lent to the land as well. In other words, the bonds were more easily broken, and syncretic mechanisms reconciling the old and the new were not so essential.

The second group to convert to Islam within the Western Sahel seem to have been elements of the urban population, and again a practical explanation can be proposed to account for this – specifically, that they might have benefited from preferable trade conditions with Muslim co-religionists, or alternatively that Islam had an appeal within the urban environment through its ability to provide cohesiveness due to the notion of community (*ummah*) which underpins it. This is a factor of potential significance in overcoming ethnic differences, which were perhaps more manifest in towns through the predilection of their very form to throw together a variety of different ethnic, social and other groups (see Insoll 2003). Again, the development of syncretic mechanisms to reconcile the old with the new appears not to have been a pressing concern.

It is also apparent that the last group to convert to Islam were the sedentary agriculturalists, the bulk of the population. Here, a feasible interpretation to explain this apparent tardiness in conversion would seem to be one related to the types of conceptual change just described; that is, the collision of different calendrical and temporal systems, which more than just prescribing when crops might be sown or harvested provided the whole framework by which being was structured. Linked with this was the concept of the ancestors, something already referred to as of potentially lesser significance for nomads in the region, and here a somewhat safer ascription as an element of traditional religious belief than is perhaps the case for the European neolithic!

Ancestral bonds and frameworks linking human and land were negotiated primarily through the construct of relationships, 'whether with other living people, or with the spirits of the dead, or with animals, or with cleared land, or with the bush' (Ranger 1991: 109). These were in turn manifest through what Ranger (ibid.) terms 'cults', as in the maintenance of cults of the land for example. The existence of the whole ancestral framework of belief and associated practices meant that breaking with or altering the balance which it sustained through conversion to Islam might have been an immensely difficult conceptual undertaking, as Bravmann (1974), for instance, has argued. To adapt a point made by Aubrey Burl (1981: 41) regarding the European neolithic to this context, 'the world was small, intense and fearsome and in it the dead were powerful'.

Hence, even though Islam might be well established within the urban environment and among nomad groups, its impact within the remainder of the rural environment was frequently minimal even several hundred years later. This can be indicated archaeologically in various ways, as in the persistence of non-Muslim burial practices such as the continuation of a tradition of urn burial in a contracted position accompanied by grave goods such as the iron bracelets and ankle-rings (Bedaux 1976: 41) found at the site of Toguere Doupwil in the Inland Niger Delta area of Mali. This was evidence dated to the fifteenth century CE, and thus long after conversion to Islam had occurred in the urban centres in the region, a process starting in the ninth–tenth centuries. Similarly, the perseverance of production of anthropomorphic and figural terracotta statuettes, contrary to Islamic proscription on the replication of figurative imagery, continues to be found up to and even beyond a similar date.

At the urban centre of Jenne-jeno, for example, also in the same region of Mali, over seventy animal or human representations have been recovered, interpreted as functioning in various ways, including for protection and in 'ancestor worship' (McIntosh and McIntosh 1979: 52) – interpretations apparently based upon ethnography, oral tradition and parallels with material from elsewhere in the region.

Where conversion did take place, syncretism of Islamic and traditional religions frequently occurred, seemingly as a mechanism for reconciling issues such as the collision of frameworks of time and their associated implications for conceptions of land: its links with people and ancestors, issues of possession, fertility, and the like. However, this is something largely indicated through ethnography, and by oral and written historical sources. Archaeology has still to make a significant impact to our understanding of syncretism in this region, primarily because of a lack of relevant research rather than it necessarily being a reflection of an absence of evidence. It could be asked, then, what the signifiers of the syncretic process are? The simple answer is that it can be all of the types of practice and belief already described within the preceding discussion of African traditional religions, fused with, to a greater or lesser extent, Islamic practice (for the latter, see Insoll 1999a). To enumerate a check list of syncretic manifestations in the West African context is pointless, diversity is profound, and what is present will depend upon individual context. Instead the important point to make is that the potential for the investigation of such phenomena undoubtedly exists in almost all contexts where religion is manifest archaeologically. Equally, similar potential exists in revisiting our notions about conversion processes, which are too frequently modelled in terms of a linear rolling out of a uniform religious type via an identical process – complexity is again denied.

It is also essential to note that the numinous element for conversion to Islam within the model just proposed has not really been broached; that is, the factor of genuine belief in Islam. This is because it is plainly irretrievable; it is irreducible, but should be recognised as a factor of probable critical importance as well, trade conditions, familiarity and ancestral cults aside. Equally, the recognition of the numinous as irretrievable also exposes how the narrative within the model just described is built upon foundations of community scale analysis; the broad sweep of nomads, town-dwellers and sedentary agriculturalists being invoked as if these were amorphous entities devoid of individuals therein. Obviously, this is not the case, but to attempt a model of such fine-grained definition as might be desired based upon the individual perspective is again, unfortunately, largely an impossibility based upon the data currently available, excluding, for instance, some data recoverable from tombstones which can signal much more than X was buried in Y. Yet this does not mean that we should not strive for such a perspective and at the very least acknowledge that it exists.

Similar more nuanced conversion models invoking syncretism as a possible adaptive mechanism, and based in part on archaeological data, have been developed for other contexts. Eaton (1993), for example, has correspondingly looked at the issue of conversion to Islam from Hinduism in Bengal. Here, he makes the important point that the term 'conversion' is difficult to apply for 'it ordinarily connotes a sudden and total transformation in which a prior religious identity is wholly rejected and replaced by a new one' (ibid.: 269). As in West Africa this is patently not the case. Change occurs slowly, and Eaton suggests three phases by which it takes place (ibid.):

- *Inclusion* – 'the process by which Islamic superhuman agencies become accepted in local Bengali cosmologies alongside local divinities therein'.
- *Identification* – Islam is merged with Bengali concepts, 'as when the Arabic name Allah was used interchangeably with the Sanskrit Niranjan'.
- *Displacement* – local gods are replaced by Islam.

Now such broad categories can be questioned in their universal application. The movement from one phase to another in a smooth linear sequence is highly unlikely, as one could get the continuation, conceivably, of pockets of 'inclusion' to the present. However, it is useful in indicating, first, how syncretism is a factor which must be included as of great relevance in thinking about such processes, and second, that 'conversion' as a very concept needs revisiting in its definitional attribution – the latter thus being added to the long list of terms we have already isolated as problematic and too frequently glibly applied.

In this instance Islam and Hinduism coincide or collide as religions, but so do their associated calendrical and temporal systems. The Islamic one has already been outlined; the Hindu one is equally complex. This is described by Walshe and Warrier (1997: 12) as 'based primarily on the lunar cycle but adapted to solar reckoning'. The oldest form of the calendar is known from texts dating from *c.* 1000 BCE and divides 'a solar year of approximately 360 days into 12 lunar months', but to align with a solar year of 365 days 'a leap month was intercalated every 60 months' (ibid.). Here, and bearing in mind that these are examples from known, living, religions, if one calendrical system was to be overlain or enmeshed syncretically with the other the complexity would greatly increase. Equally, it can also be seen that if we as archaeologists were to treat Hindu and Islamic time solely as secular and linear alone we would be failing comprehensively in our interpretations. How often might this have been done for the past?

Yet this does not mean that syncretism only appears at the interface of world and traditional religions. This is not so, syncretism occurs 'at every point in the course of religious life' (Eliade 1958: 462). This said, its most easily investigative point of entry might be within what could be termed 'religious fracture zones', but these are by no means static. The blending, fusion, the syncretism of old and new religious belief and practice have happened continually, and archaeology is well placed to investigate this, though again anthropology provides a useful illustrative example of what is meant by this. For Wendy James's (1988) study of the Uduk of the southern Funj area of the Sudan indicates the power of syncretism as a conceptual tool in approaching the complexities of religion. Amongst this ethnic group, numbering only some 10,000 people, religion 'is like a pattern of sand-dunes partially obscured beneath a shifting sea; what has been lost at one time, may be found by someone else in another place, when the sea later retreats . . . The fundamental substance is always there, beneath the surface waves; but its elements are continually shifting and rearranging themselves' (ibid.: 270).

Practically, this has meant that since the turn of the twentieth century, as well as retaining elements they define as culturally theirs in origin, the Uduk have 'appropriated' elements of religious practice – healing cults, oracles, festivals – from neighbouring ethnic groups such as the Shilluk and Nuer, and have also shown periodic enthusiasm for both Islam and Christianity. An instance of the former is described by James (ibid.: 259) who recounts how in 1953 many Uduk men converted to Islam only to abandon it equally rapidly the following year. Now here, it could be argued, the circumstances are exceptional, the Uduk being located on one of these aforementioned borderlands or religious and ethnic fracture zones, allied with the fact that the twentieth century was a period of exceptional change and exposure to world 'events'. The applicability of all these factors can certainly be debated, but it is unnecessary to do this here. Rather it can be suggested that it is more probable that the types of religious syncretism, fusion, and abandonment processes evident among the Uduk are not atypical but more common than we think, and archaeology is well placed to consider such issues, concerned as it usually is with longer-term timescales – but timescales which should often be considered as generated by dynamic, fluid processes and not representative of stasis *per se*.

The intermixing of symbols from different religious systems offers a way into evaluating this through material culture, but again caution has to be exercised. Reading the symbols is by no means simple; their meanings can change or be lost owing to syncretism, fusion or rejection. Koloss (n.d.: 124–5), for instance, describes how in the nineteenth century European explorers and scientific missions entering the Congo region found the relics of slaving and missionary campaigns linked with Portuguese contact with the Kingdom of Kongo between the late fifteenth and eighteenth centuries. The material legacy of these contacts included devotional images, crucifixes and rosaries made by local craftsmen, but the 'original meaning of these objects had long been forgotten, and they now served as magic charms or royal insignia' (ibid.). In this instance it can be suggested that it was hardly the loving Christ which was represented on the crucifixes, but the symbol of some vague foreign oppressor whose origins and significance must have been associated with fear and power in oral memory.

Both of the examples just described, in recognising that world religions can be abandoned as well as accepted, stand in contrast to many older models developed in reference to West African material such as that considered earlier where conversion to Islam was seen as an advance, a development from the earlier 'pagan' belief systems which existed; thus giving up Islam would have been interpreted within such a paradigm as a retrograde step. Within Francophone West Africa for example, the origins of the great 'medieval' empires, which were amongst the first polities to be exposed to Islam in sub-Saharan Africa, were sought outside of Africa. Thus individuals such as Maurice Delafosse (1922) argued that Ghana, the first of these empires, was 'founded and ruled by Judeo-Syrians from the fourth to eighth centuries AD' (De Barros 1990: 161). Archaeologically, this meant that colonial focus in this region was upon the capitals of the empires, sites that could be tied to Arab texts, and hence the civilising effects of Islam were promoted in subsequent interpretation.

Such evolutionary conceptions of the impact of Islam were rooted within the particular circumstances of French West Africa, and Augustine Holl (1996: 139) has described how French colonial scholarship served to provide data up the chain of command, allowing those at the top to use this for grand interpretation 'of the historical precedence and superiority of white people over black natives, thus reinforcing their *mission civilisatrice*'. The influential French archaeologist Raymond Mauny (1961: 390), for instance, drew parallels between settlements such as Koumbi Saleh, the reputed capital of the empire of Ghana, and the neighbouring trade centre of Tegdaoust, in Mauritania, and the manner in which European cities were superimposed next to the medinas of the colonial Maghreb. Hence, consciously or subconsciously, archaeologists of the colonial period were thereby justifying their own presence. Colonisation had occurred before, thus they were only continuing a long tradition (Insoll 2003). Archaeology and religion were here intertwined to serve what were in effect secular political ends.

## Categorisation

We have moved away from syncretism and it is to here that we should return in briefly noting that religious fusion and syncretism are perhaps far more frequent than often considered, for the obsession of categorization denies what Barnes (1997a: 11) aptly defines as 'bi-religiosity'. Within our archaeology of religions we need to explore more fully the notions of syncretism and religious dualism, of multiple elements comfortably co-existing as we saw with the Yoruba example, and in so doing defying neat categories. Queer archaeology (Dowson 2000) can be extended into the domain of the archaeological study of religions if it helps us to acknowledge complexity and the 'other'. The prevailing desire for classification can in fact be wholly inappropriate. Where do the boundaries of Islam cease and those of African traditional religion begin for instance? Archaeology allows us to consider such classificatory categories – not as an exercise in reinforcing their existence but rather in indicating their permeability.

The obsession with classification which is found has already been described and numerous examples exist of the inappropriate classification of religion. Within an African context such classificatory conundrums relate to whether the term 'African traditional religion' or 'African traditional religions' in the plural is used. The overall term of African traditional religion/religions was developed, rightly, as a counter to demeaning labels such as 'paganism', 'fetishism', 'animism' or 'magic' which were formerly applied to describe religious practices in Africa (Mbiti 1991: 18–19). However, although well-intentioned in origin, its use in the singular is inappropriate, this term being generated, as Rosalind Shaw (1990: 339) notes, from 'the paradigmatic status accorded in religious studies to the Judeo-Christian tradition and of the associated view of "religion as text"'. 'African traditional religions' is preferable for it describes a complex of varying elements, such as those described for the Yoruba or Dogon, which may or may not be present, and which lack a spurious pan-continental ascription, as argued, for example, by Zeusse (1991: 171) who although using the plural, mentions that African traditional religions are 'merely local variations on a few axiomatic themes'. However, rather than emphasising timelessness and similarity, change and a historical dimension have to be acknowledged in African traditional religions, as Ranger (1991: 109) has described, for 'the metaphorical and ritual language of religion, so far from reiterating changelessness, is the very form which change takes'.

Another example of a similarly misused term of non-'world' religious application is provided by the label 'totemism', which, according to Lévi-Strauss ([1962] 1991: 24), has frequently been hastily used, and is a label which does not do justice to 'the extreme complexity and heterogeneous character of beliefs and customs' (ibid.) contained therein. Furthermore, 'animism' too is commonly also wrongly defined and applied – privileged as an actual religion when in reality it might, and often does, refer to an element within a larger system, as was described with reference to Yoruba practice earlier.

Yet perhaps one of the most contentious of religious terms which is used is 'shaman' and its collective term 'shamanism'. As has already been noted, archaeological investigations of shamanism are polarised, and this extends into definition as well. Price (2001: 4) describes the process by which the term 'shaman' came into popular usage: how the Tungus word 'Sâman' became known to the outside world after a dissident Russian Orthodox priest entered Siberia in the mid-seventeenth century. However, 'shamanism' as a 'notion of a collective pattern of belief' (ibid.) began after Christian missions started targeting Siberia and sought to create a pagan 'other' which they could Christianise (and see Kehoe 2000: 101). Hence it would appear that here we have the same sort of definitional problem as that already described – the inappropriate creation of a religious 'identity' where such an ascription might not actually be relevant.

Criticisms of this process of shamanic 'creation', but more so of the subsequent application of ill-thought-out shamanic definitions, are various (see, for example, Kehoe 2000; Bahn 2001; Helvenston and Bahn 2002). Hutton (2001: 51) makes the relevant point, in reviewing the foundations of shamanism in its supposed Siberian heartland, that even here it 'was not a single functional phenomenon'. Mircea Eliade ([1964] 1989), almost the founding father of contemporary shamanic definition, has also been extensively criticised, as for example by Kehoe (2000: 39–41), for generalising about what shamanism is, not completing any relevant fieldwork which might assist in formulating the required definition, and utilising an approach invoking 'cultural primitivism'. His use of trance – the 'archaic techniques of ecstasy' (Eliade [1964] 1989) – as a defining characteristic of shamanism is also picked out for criticism (Kehoe 2000; and see Bahn 2001: 55) as something frequently jumped upon by other scholars as a distinguishing feature; hence if present it is used to interpret the presence of shamans where none might in fact have existed.

Certainly, many of these criticisms are valid. As was described in Chapter 2, shamans are now routinely identified under almost every 'archaeological stone', but it could also be suggested that the debate over what constitutes shamanism, and its associated archaeological investigation, has reached a point of such division of opinion that it has ceased to be constructive, and that in order to begin to define what the shaman and shamanism actually is, a step back from acrimony needs to be taken and the definitional evidence revisited before we can begin to break the types of rigidly held notions that shamans and shamanism are alternatively:

- Indefinable.
- A general phenomenon which 'may be broadly defined as someone who somehow specialises in mediating between

the spiritual and social on behalf of society through the use of specialist techniques and specialist knowledge' (Strassburg 2000: 78).

- Associated predominantly with northern Eurasia and bordering areas such as North America (Hultkrantz 1978: 55).

Here, archaeology could contribute in constructively reassessing the definition of 'shaman' and 'shamanism' by concentrating upon a contextualised approach to the data whereby an attempt could be made to look at all facets of the evidence, as has already been discussed, where available. Hence, for instance, rock art, a favourite source of evidence for shamanic interpretations (see, for example, Clottes and Lewis-Williams 1998; Lewis-Williams 2002), would not necessarily be left floating but instead could be placed within its overall archaeological framework (Figure 8). So that, for example, upper palaeolithic rock art and cave sanctuaries would not be defined as shamanic primarily on the basis

*Figure 8* Rock engraving, Wadi Madkandoush, Libya. Object of fear, tasty meal, totemic emblem, early naturalists' interest? (photo T. Insoll)

of that source of evidence alone, but with the settlement evidence and burial evidence, indeed all facets of the evidence, being taken into account when building the composite picture of religious identity.

Thus in the end we might come to realise that the search for a 'pure' describable shamanism is the root of the problem in that it is but one element fused with various others in forming the composite religious identity, rather than being the overall religious identity itself. For the people in the European upper palaeolithic, mesolithic, neolithic, African Late Stone Age or whatever, are extremely unlikely to have called their religious specialists 'shamans' and to have described themselves as followers of 'shamanism'. The 'shaman' might be the interpretatively fashionable religious label of the moment, but it too would seem to be, in the majority of its applications, a miscategorisation, a reduction of something infinitely more complex to a label which is, even in its relatively recent creation, little understood in itself.

'Hinduism' provides another example of religious categorisation which can be briefly explored, in this instance rooted within the context of world religions (Insoll 2001a). This religious label is examined in some detail by Von Stietencron (1989: 11), who indicates how 'Hindu' is a Persian variant of the Sanskrit *sindhu*, the Indus river, meaning in the plural 'the population living in that region: the Indus people, the Indians'. It is a term used with some precision by Persian scholars who could recognise various different religions among the Hindus after Muslim settlement in the Indus Valley from 712 CE, but which began to lose definition after the later arrival of Europeans who used 'Hindoo' as a classification of the 'non-Muslim masses of India without these scholarly differentiations' (ibid.: 12). In effect a single classificatory category, 'Hinduism', a religion, was created out of a mass of diversity within, and equally is a term which it can be suggested in part persists as it serves better national claims within India rooted around 'Hindu' politics strengthened by notions of unity rather than diversity. Perhaps 'Hindu religions' is, as Von Stietencron (ibid.: 20) notes, a better label to define this group of related yet different traditions.

These examples of the mislabelling of religions would appear to be a reflection of the classificatory conundrum, which Needham (1975: 365) would refer to as the presumption of the existence of monothetic classes of social facts when in reality their point of reference is polythetic. As already noted, much of the material we deal with crosses categories and as such is analogous with Foucault's ([1970] 2002: 160) notion of 'intermediate productions', with his apt examples being 'the flying squirrel between the bird and the quadruped, the monkey between the quadruped and man'. The classification of religions can serve, as Geertz (1968: 24) notes, 'toward denaturing our material, toward substituting cliché for description and assumption for analysis'.

As mentioned, archaeology offers an ideal way of reassessing categorisation (Insoll forthcoming a), and a way of cracking the preoccupation with religious classification and categories might be to consider what Barnes (1997a: 13) describes as Wittgenstein's theory of 'family resemblances' (1953), which has been in turn translated into the methodology of 'polythetic classification' (Needham 1975). It is inadvisable to make the mistake of promoting this as a panacea for understanding the complex character of religions; its utility lies within looking for overlapping similarities/resemblances rather than 'monotypic' (Barnes 1997a: 13) features. Numerous theoretical examples of its potential use could be suggested where seeking resemblances might facilitate looking at the development of a religion, or conversion to a religion in a particular context.

Barnes (ibid.) reduces the idea of polythetic classification to the following diagrammatic structure:

ABCD
AB DE
A CDE
BC EF

This is interpreted as lacking a monotypic feature within all the sets, but 'there is sufficient overlap in the features of each set to establish a family or a chain of overlapping resemblances' (ibid.).

This interpretation is fair, and we can adapt it for our purposes with reference to the particular case study being considered here. For example:

African Traditional Religions – Islam – Christianity
African Traditional Religions – Islam    Christianity
Islam    African Traditional Religions – Christianity

Resemblances can be sought between the materials under investigation, and such a perspective also helps in dismantling the notion of the 'great' and 'little' traditions critiqued earlier. Instead the possibility of similarity is considered and if need be discarded. Yet as with all the examples included, the necessity of applying a multidisciplinary approach, wherever possible, must again be stressed in attempting to implement a holistic perspective, which has already been described as a prerequisite in developing a meaningful archaeology of religion which obviously has as a part of its remit approaches to religious categorisation, syncretism and time. In summary, the case study just considered indicates the power of archaeology as a means of assessing not only the impact of religion, but the very nature of religion itself.

# 5

# PROSPECTS AND CONCLUSION

This book has by necessity been critical in tone, for only by dismantling existing archaeological approaches to religion can we attempt to rebuild a more coherent archaeology of religions. Furthermore, it is hoped that the adoption of a critical approach to existing research will stimulate much-needed debate concerning this neglected area of archaeological endeavour both within and – it is optimistically further added – outside our discipline. For in this respect a key point to re-emphasise is that a presumption of archaeological 'ownership' of the relevant data and debate produces a non-starter from the outset. If anything, the archaeological study of religion demands an interdisciplinary or multidisciplinary approach.

## Prospects

Yet pessimism and self-reflection aside, it must be stated that the prospects for the future of the archaeology of religion look promising because:

- the necessary re-evaluation of theoretical and practical approaches is beginning to be undertaken;
- much new and relevant research is being completed in many areas and on many periods;

- there is an increasing realisation that the archaeology of religion is, or should be, concerned with a wider range of evidence than previously considered;

- the archaeology of religion is a vast field but one which can also now be considered as coming into its own rather than as an afterthought to other issues usually considered by archaeologists: settlement, demography, economy, political structures, etc.

As noted previously, religion itself is increasingly being (re)-recognised as of importance within the 'secular' West, a realisation which has profound implications for archaeology, considering the proportional impact of Western archaeologists on archaeological theory, interpretation and methodology. Here we need to recognise that our concepts of being are flawed unless we acknowledge religion as a potentially critical element of past being. Equally, in recognising such, archaeologists do not somehow have to commit to religion. Yet secular, agnostic, atheist outlooks seem to structure views on past religiosity, and the great strides which our discipline has made in many other areas of investigation have yet to be reflected within archaeology and religion – one of our last 'virgin' frontiers of archaeological theorising. In so doing, religion might actually be recognised as a significant domain of past activity by archaeologists, rather than the 'dustbin' (Hultkrantz 1978: 27) for otherwise inexplicable data and far-fetched interpretations which it sometimes resembles at present.

## A future approach? Towards a theory of archaeology and religion?

### A return to Dafra

It is also necessary to suggest how we might begin to approach the archaeological study of religion, and here, first, it is useful to return to the example of the sacred forest and shrine at Dafra in Burkina Faso described in the Prologue. This is because it contains within it many of the material elements, definitional conundrums, theoretical issues and research questions identified as encompassed within the archaeology of religion. These include:

1 *Visibility.* This is as expressed in the natural versus the human altered elements of the setting. Although a natural place it is undeniably altered by human action, as indicated by the protection of the catfish, vultures and vegetation, or by the creation of the fireplace, ash and feathers (carcasses and hence faunal remains are predominantly removed for consumption by the priest and his family), and the paths leading to the shrine littered with broken pots and other detritus left by people travelling to and from there.

2 *Definition.* The very definition, 'shrine', can be seen to be again inappropriate. Here, it has been used to refer to the stone pillar (a semantic point not necessarily agreed with by this author, but useful as a descriptive device commonly understood). But equally, it could be applied to the sacred forest, and all the other elements therein within the definitional parameters popularly understood as encompassed by the term 'shrine'. 'Shrine' thus lacks clarity.

3 *Myth.* Myth as seemingly interwoven in the origins of this sacred place. Historically, it is thought to have risen to prominence during a period of instability associated with events in the Kenedougou kingdom of Sikasso in the eighteenth century (S. Berthe, pers. comm.). But its origins are the subject of myth, which though expressed as a factor of importance to this author were not outlined. Yet in pursuing the myth in the future we should also recognise that we have to also tease out the interwoven strands of historical tradition, both oral, and potentially written, the whole largely completed within the framework of ethnographic study – our interdisciplinary or multidisciplinary connections are again evident.

4 *Ritual.* Evident in the repetitious formalised nature of actions within the shrine area as described. It incorporates movement (into and out of the gorge, within the sacred forest), noise (knocking, calling fish), sensory alteration (light/shade), and emotional stimulation (prayer, sacrifice). It includes ritual

148

action which engages with both mind and body, inseparably, and ritual action which is completed by the individual, but within the group.

5   *Time.* As expressed at an individual level through the completion of the ritual actions, but also as projected into the future through the notion of return, foresworn if successful in the presence of the shrine. Time as also encapsulated in the very existence of this traditional sacred place within an area likewise subject to Christian and Islamic time-frames as well. Also as manifest in different 'strata': the long-term forces, *'la longue-durée'*, of enduring sacrality; the medium-term *'conjonctures'* of changing ritual action and custodianship; the *'evenements'* or 'fireflies' (Braudel 1972: 901) of time as reflected, for example, in myriad individual visits.

6   *Syncretism/identity.* The ritual actions are completed by Muslims, Christians and followers of traditional religions (the distinction between which is often also blurred). The shrine might be under the guardianship of Bobo followers of traditional religion, but exclusivity is not expressed in who might visit and participate in rituals there. Yet as we have seen syncretism has also to be recognised as extremely complex, and, as well as being testified materially, is also a mental construct where different weighting could be lent to different religious elements depending upon individual disposition; this too underpins ritual practice at Dafra.

7   *Belief/emotion/experience.* Why complete the ritual? Why do people do it? It defies rationality, but people genuinely believe that it will bring results, or alternatively feel curious enough to undergo the experience of completing the ritual. Both often accompanied by visible emotion – fear, awe, relief, happiness.

8   *The numinous/the holy.* The shrine is but one rock among many within one gorge among many that happens to be set within a piece of relic forest. This might be a correct description of the significance of the boulder and its setting, but there is obviously much more to it. Yet the question needs to be asked: how to describe this? As a universal experience of the sacred/holiness, or at an individual level? Furthermore,

is the atmosphere/significance of the shrine really possible to describe? The answer to the former is both, and the answer to the latter, ultimately, negative.

## Final words

In the end, although we can isolate multiple elements surrounding the shrine at Dafra, as an archaeological site stripped of the perspective of contemporary participation/observation from which the account in the Prologue of the book is constructed, much of this would elude us. We are very unlikely to retrieve anything of the rich text which surrounds and creates it, a text which is only partial as no attempt has been made to slot this shrine and its accompanying ritual into the wider framework of Bobo life and belief. The shrine and any ritual completed within it would soon be effaced. 'Thick description' is to be desired and striven for as much as possible but the true answer is that we need to recognise the existence of numinous and irreducible elements as well. In so doing this is essentially providing the necessary recognition that elements of the archaeology of religions are metaphysical by definition. Unfortunately, with much of the archaeology of religions we will never get at its essence no matter how long we boil the pot, because it is in the mind, it defies rationality, and the best-meant assertions of cognitive processualism aside, it will remain elusive.

However, we do need to approach religion as a possible component underlying all the use and meaning of material culture – not only as a term applied to 'ritual objects'. We need to recognise the potentially embedded nature of religion as a key building block, if not sometimes *the* key building block of identity. For as has been stressed such an approach allows religion to be seen as part of a holistic package possibly structuring all aspects of life, with 'religious' material culture being seen as a very ambiguous category which is very difficult to define. Do we exclude material which might have been used while people entertained religious thoughts, the underlying intention of which we can

150

never reconstruct? Or do we only include a pre-determined check-list of materials 'definitely' religious in intent?

Ambiguity is preferred here and emphasis is placed upon 'possibility'. Nevertheless, to begin to understand how all-pervading the influence of religion might be on material culture its conceptualisation needs to be shifted from explicit contexts of a ritual/'strange' nature to a much larger and broader framework. This, if anything, is the required conceptual or theoretical shift. Hence the extent to which 'religiosity' influenced life and material culture will vary, but we can begin to approach it by looking at religion as existing in multiple contexts, and by looking at the overall context.

This, in part, offers a way to begin to approach an 'archaeological' Dafra, through not only focusing upon the shrine and its gorge but also by attempting to reconstruct the whole package of the archaeology of Bobo religion. To look at one element alone and to take this as the benchmark for a religious life is wrong and would perpetuate the usually posited association that ritual = strange, the hypothetical scenario of perfect preservation giving 'strange' catfish, lots of chicken remains, a bloodied pillar, an emphasis upon water. But these elements are just that, 'elements', placed within a religion which structures many other facets of Bobo life (see, for example, Cremer 1924; Le Moal 1980) and in which these 'strange' elements make sense only as small parts of a much wider whole. To begin to unravel this in archaeological contexts we have to look for the wider contextual associations of shrines plus houses plus funerary practices plus diet plus agricultural practices plus technology plus landscape alteration and perception, and so on.

We also need to focus on time as a mechanism for approaching the archaeology of religions. Time is obviously crucial but has been largely ignored, as noted, by archaeologists. Yet time can be restructured by religions (as in the examples already considered); it can be layered and superimposed in the ritual cycle. This not only invokes the presumed definable 'sacred' time of festivals, Eliade's ahistorical 'primordial mythical time made present' (1959: 69) but also involves a recognition of all the complexities inherent in the collision and superimposition of different temporal cycles. Hence time should not only be conceived of by archaeologists as comprising processual profane time, but also religious time which can structure and alter life.

Similarly, the potency of religion as an agent for ethnic or language change has yet to be fully explored. The archaeology of linguistics or ethnicity might be considered (Renfrew 1989; Jones 1997), but the potential fundamental role of religion within the processes which we as archaeologists consider with regard to these key signifiers of identity has yet to be fully measured. Thus, for example, in reviewing scholarship pertaining to the changes of ethnic boundaries and identity which can take place, Jones (1997: 110) indicates that this has predominantly been assessed with regard to the 'strategic manipulation of identity with relation to economic and political relations'. The absence of religion within such mechanisms of ethnicity and identity change is an omission, and a similar point can be made with reference to language change. The crucial role of Arabic within the Islamic world provides a case in point, where because of its especial status it theoretically has the potential to supplant other languages through its divine attributes. Equally, these are issues of potential applicability outside literate world religious archaeological contexts, for a need to conform, for instance, desired or achieved under duress, but generated from a religious perspective, could likewise exist in prehistoric contexts as well.

Likewise, gender, though neglected within this volume, is also of crucial significance within the archaeology of religions. This does not mean the pursuit of a stereotypical 'female' role within 'explicitly' religious contexts – a pursuit of the 'nuns of prehistory' for example – but rather a recognition that the role of gender can be profound in structuring the material which we consider. Religion can both generate and maintain gender relations; it can also provide the structure for all gender relations – as within Islamic practice for instance. More fundamentally, ignoring or subsuming gender within some form of 'genderless' entity can, conceivably, have profound implications. Diane Bell, in discussing women's ritual among Aboriginal groups in Central Australia, makes the relevant point that here,

> where male and female worlds are substantially indepen-
> dent of one another in economic and ritual terms, men
> and women elaborate gender-specific power bases. The
> cultural ramifications of the separation of the sexes are
> so far-reaching that they preclude one from evaluating
> or comparing the contribution of each sex to their society
> within one domain.
>
> (Bell 1993: 23)

Thus it is not only recognition that might be required, but also an appreciation of the potential of gender and its implications for religion in 'tandem' so to speak – as different worlds can be constructed from gender 'foundations' and hence co-exist cognitively, and by implication, materially.

We also need to think of our scale of analysis – individual, communal, universal. In other words we need to have both our cake and eat it, proverbially speaking. The importance of the concept of the individual and the impact of the Enlightenment upon many archaeologists, and others' concepts of this, and of religion, has been critiqued. Yet in the same way, both the recognition of the individual, individual agency, and individual critical perspective should not be suppressed. Nonetheless, both the individual and larger-scale frameworks of analysis need acknowledging within the archaeology of religion, both the individual and the 'universal bodies' (Fowler 2000: 114), entailing the difficult conflation of a variety of approaches, theoretical and methodological.

What is required is what Scruton (2002: 257) discusses in outlining the philosopher Gottleb Frege's thesis 'On Sense and Reference'. Namely, 'that it is only in the context of a whole sentence that a word has a definite meaning; second, that the meaning of any sentence must be derivable from the meaning of its parts'. This is precisely the seemingly contradictory conundrum which the archaeology of religion necessitates, which, translated for our purpose, is the emphasis upon context in its individual and communal forms – both are required for us to ever begin to reconstruct relevant past meaning.

Ritual, for example, functions at both a community and at an individual/personal level; we, as archaeologists, need to consider both in a holistic contextual manner. Suppressing desires to reconstruct the meaning of, for example, communal neolithic religion based upon a supposed 'experience' of what ritual entailed in a handful of tombs or causewayed enclosures, but at the same time pushing at the frontiers of our discipline so that we can begin to chart what Zeusse (1987: 409) terms 'the ritual field of correspondences and boundaries', is an entry point into understanding 'to what degree ritual is a mediation on the final and basic experiences of the body', which to adapt the point made by Zeusse (ibid.), should mean both the personal and the communal body(ies).

Certainly, one relevant 'body'-related research possibility is presented by the potential emphasis upon the right side which might be evident within ritual, and therefore, for instance, perhaps manifest in the structuring of sacred space. This is not a suggestion underlain by universalising post- or neo-structuralist purpose, but rather generated by the possibilities offered by the role of the right hand and its links with conceptions of purity as extensively explored by Hertz (1973: 120), who describes the emphasis placed upon the right as fit for 'beneficial relations' with the gods. Whilst standing in opposition the left prevails in the domain of 'containing or appeasing spiteful or angry supernatural beings, (or) to banishing or destroying bad influences' (ibid.: 121). Indeed, ritual as a whole needs to be reconsidered as more than the action of otherwise 'strange' or unexplained intent by archaeologists; rather it is the reflection of normative action, albeit frequently structured with divine objective, for it is this which sets it apart from merely repetitive action.

Equally, we need constantly to revisit our assumptions regarding religious definitions. Throughout it has been emphasised how our accepted definitions can be weak and inappropriate: religion itself; the alternatives which are euphemistically applied by archaeologists, 'ritual', 'cult', 'spirituality', etc.; religious 'types' (world versus traditional, for instance), animism, totemism, shamanism, Hinduism – all are labels which have been evaluated and their weaknesses indicated. The strait-jacket of classification is a limiting factor and it was suggested that one way to begin to address this is to think in terms of family resemblances rather than binding types. Here our discipline, archaeology, can make a significant contribution in indicating the complexities which have existed in terms both of religious forms themselves and the nature of overlapping religious identities. To achieve this a multidisciplinary approach is vital. Archaeologists should draw upon as many sources of evidence as possible, as already illustrated with regard to the case studies, but without the presumed arrogance of attempting to apply a supra-disciplinary approach, the flaw of history of religions, as also already critiqued.

Finally, the weaknesses of the argument in approaching a subject as complex as the archaeology of religions are all too apparent to this author. A charge of religious determinism and idealism might be levelled at this study – wrongly, for ultimately a theoretical, definitional and methodological shift is required by archaeologists in how they approach this poor cousin of archaeological research. Yet ultimately we have to recognise that our insight into religion through archaeology, at best, will only be partial; a 'theory' of archaeology and religion is elusive. We cannot achieve the seemingly demanded pre-Enlightenment, pre-modernity perspective which might sometimes be desirable. We are limited by the awe-inspiring creature which is religion(s) – irreducible and complex – and we need at least to acknowledge this.

# BIBLIOGRAPHY

Achaya, K.T. 1994. *Indian Food. A Historical Companion*. Delhi: Oxford University Press.

Adediran, A.A. 1992. The Early Beginnings of the Ife State. In Akinjogbin, I.A. (ed.), *The Cradle of a Race. Ife*. Port Harcourt, Nigeria: Sunray, pp. 77–95.

Adediran, A.A. and Arifalo, S.O. 1992. The Religious Festivals of Ife. In Akinjogbin, I.A. (ed.), *The Cradle of a Race. Ife*. Port Harcourt, Nigeria: Sunray, pp. 305–17.

Allen, D. 1987. Phenomenology of Religion. In Eliade, M. (ed.), *The Encyclopedia of Religion*. London: Macmillan, pp. 272–85.

Anderson, S. and Boyle, K. 1996. *Ritual Treatment of Human and Animal Remains*. Oxford: Oxbow Books.

Anon. 1972. Foreword. In Marx, K. and Engels, F. *On Religion*. Moscow: Progress Publishers.

Antanaitis, I. 1998. Interpreting the Meaning of Eastern Baltic Neolithic symbols. *Cambridge Archaeological Journal* 8: 55–68.

Awolalu, J.O. 1979. *Yoruba Beliefs and Sacrificial Rites*. London: Longman.

Bahn, P. 1996. Comment. *Cambridge Archaeological Journal* 6: 55–7.

Bahn, P. 2001. Save the Last Trance for Me: An Assessment of the Misuse of Shamanism in Rock Art Studies. In Francfort, H.-P. and Hamayon, R.N. (eds), *The Concept of Shamanism: Uses and Abuses*. Budapest: Akadémiai Kiadó, pp. 51–94.

Bailey, G. 1983. Concepts of Time in Quaternary Prehistory. *Annual Review of Anthropology* 12: 165–92.

Barnes, S. 1997a. The Many Faces of Ogun. In Barnes, S. (ed.), *Africa's Ogun. Old World and New*. Bloomington: Indiana University Press, pp. 1–26.

Barnes, S. 1997b. Africa's Ogun Transformed. In Barnes, S. (ed.), *Africa's Ogun. Old World and New*. Bloomington: Indiana University Press, pp. xiii–xxi.

Basilov, V.N. 1984. The Study of Shamanism in Soviet Ethnography. In Hoppál, M. (ed.), *Shamanism in Eurasia*. Göttingen: Edition Herodot, pp. 46–63.

Bastide, R. 1978. *The African Religions of Brazil*. Baltimore, Md.: Johns Hopkins University Press.

Bean, L.J. 1992. Introduction. In Bean, L.J. (ed.), *California Indian Shamanism*. Menlo Park, Calif.: Ballena Press, pp. 1–6.

Bean, L.J. and Vane, S.B. 1992. The Shamanic Experience. In Bean, L.J. (ed.), *California Indian Shamanism*. Menlo Park, Calif.: Ballena Press, pp. 7–19.

Bedaux, R. 1972. Tellem, Reconnaissance Archéologique d'une Culture de l'Ouest Africain au Moyen-Age: Recherches Architectoniques. *Journal de la Societe des Africanistes* 42: 103–85.

Bedaux, R. 1976. Mali (Note on Excavations at Togueres Doupwil and Galia). *Nyame Akuma* 8: 40–3.

Bedaux, R. 1991. Des Tellem aux Dogon: Recherches Archéologiques dans la Boucle du Niger (Mali). *Dall' Archeologia all' arte tradizionale Africana*. Rome: Centro Studio Archeologia Africana.

Bell, C. 1992. *Ritual Theory, Ritual Practice*. Oxford: Oxford University Press.

Bell, C. 1997. *Ritual Perspectives and Dimensions*. Oxford: Oxford University Press.

Bell, D. 1993. *Daughters of the Dreaming*. London: Allen and Unwin.

Bender, B., Hamilton, S. and Tilley, C. 1997. Leskernick: Stone Worlds; Alternative Narratives; Nested Landscapes. *Proceedings of the Prehistoric Society* 63: 147–78.

Binford, L. 1962. Archaeology as Anthropology. *American Antiquity* 28: 217–25.

Binford, L. 1967. Smudge Pits and Hide Smoking: The Use of Analogy in Archaeological Reasoning. *American Antiquity* 32: 1–12.

Binford, L. 1972a. 'Red Ochre' Caches from the Michigan Area: A Possible Case of Cultural Drift. In Binford, L., *An Archaeological Perspective*. New York: Seminar Press, pp. 295–313.

Binford, L. 1972b. Mortuary Practices: Their Study and Their Potential. In Binford, L., *An Archaeological Perspective*. New York: Seminar Press, pp. 208–43.

# BIBLIOGRAPHY

Binford, L. 1978. *Nunamiut Ethnoarchaeology*. New York: Academic Press.

Binford, L. 1983. *In Pursuit of the Past*. London: Thames and Hudson.

Bogucki, P. 1999. *The Origins of Human Society*. Oxford: Blackwell.

Boivin, N. 2000. Life Rhythms and Floor Sequences: Excavating Time in Rural Rajasthan and Neolithic Catalhöyük. *World Archaeology* 31: 367–88.

Bortin, V. 1980. Science and the Shroud of Turin. *Biblical Archaeologist* (Spring): 109–17.

Bowie, F. 1998. Trespassing on Sacred Domains. A Feminist Anthropological Approach to Theology and Religious Studies. *Journal of Feminist Studies in Religion* 14: 40–62.

Bowie, F. 2000. *The Anthropology of Religion*. Oxford: Blackwell.

Boyer, P. 2001. *Religion Explained*. New York: Basic Books.

Bradley, R. 1991. Ritual, Time and History. *World Archaeology* 23: 209–19.

Bradley, R. 2000. *An Archaeology of Natural Places*. London: Routledge.

Braudel, F. 1972. *The Mediterranean and the Mediterranean World in the Age of Phillip II*. London: Collins.

Bravmann, R. 1974. *Islam and Tribal Art in West Africa*. Cambridge: Cambridge University Press.

Brück, J. 1999. Ritual and Rationality: Some Problems of Interpretation in European Archaeology. *European Journal of Archaeology* 2: 313–44.

Burl, A. 1981. *Rites of the Gods*. London: Dent.

Burl, A. 1997. *Prehistoric Astronomy and Ritual*. Princes Risborough, Bucks., UK: Shire Publications.

Byrne, P. 1988. Religion and the Religions. In Clarke, P. and Sutherland, S. (eds), *The Study of Religion, Traditional and New Religions*. London: Routledge, pp. 3–28.

Campbell, J. 1989. Foreword. In Gimbutas, M., *The Language of the Goddess*. London: Thames and Hudson, pp. xiii–xiv.

Campbell, S. and Green, A. (eds). 1995. *The Archaeology of Death in the Ancient Near East*. Oxford: Oxbow Books.

Carmichael, D., Hubert, J., Reeves, B. and Schanche, A. (eds). 1994. *Sacred Sites, Sacred Places*. London: Routledge.

Carrithers, M., Collins, S. and Lukes, S. (eds). 1985. *The Category of the Person*. Cambridge: Cambridge University Press.

Carver, M. 1993. In Search of Cult. In Carver, M. (ed.), *In Search of Cult*. Woodbridge: Boydell Press, pp. v–ix.

Cassirer, E. 1951. *The Philosophy of the Enlightenment*. Princeton, N.J.: Princeton University Press.

Chakrabarti, D. 2001. The Archaeology of Hinduism. In Insoll, T. (ed.), *Archaeology and World Religion*. London: Routledge, pp. 33–60.

Chakrabarti, S. 1999. The Mahabharata. Archaeological and Literary Evidence. In Insoll, T. (ed.), *Case Studies in Archaeology and World Religion*. BAR S755. Oxford: Archaeopress, pp. 166–74.

Chase, P. and Dibble, H. 1987. Middle Palaeolithic Symbolism: A Review of Current Evidence and Interpretations. *Journal of Anthropological Archaeology* 6: 263–96.

Chaudhuri, N.C. 1997. *Hinduism. A Religion to Live By*. Delhi: Oxford University Press.

Childe, V.G. 1945. *Progress and Archaeology*. London: Watts.

Childe, V.G. 1947. *History*. London: Cobbett Press.

Childe, V.G. 1956. *Piecing Together the Past*. London: Routledge.

Clack, T. In Press. Neurophenomenology: A Worthwhile Research Direction for the Archaeological Study of Religion? In Insoll, T. (ed.), *Trowelling Belief. The Proceedings of the Manchester Conference on Archaeology and Religion*. Oxford: Archaeopress.

Cladis, M.S. 2001. Introduction. In Durkheim, E. *The Elementary Forms of Religious Life*. Oxford: Oxford University Press, pp. vii–xxxv.

Clark, G. 1989. *World Prehistory*. Cambridge: Cambridge University Press.

Clarke, D.L. 1978. *Analytical Archaeology*. London: Methuen.

Clifford, J. 1983. Power and Dialogue in Ethnography. Marcel Griaule's Initiation. In Stocking, G. (ed.). *Observers Observed*. Madison: University of Wisconsin Press, pp. 121–56.

Clottes, J. and Lewis-Williams, D. 1998. *The Shamans of Prehistory*. New York: Harry N. Abrams.

Coningham, R. 2001. The Archaeology of Buddhism. In Insoll, T. (ed.), *Archaeology and World Religion*. London: Routledge, pp. 61–95.

Cooney, G. 1994. Sacred and Secular Neolithic landscapes. In Carmichael, D., Hubert, J., Reeves, B. and Schanche, A. (eds), *Sacred Sites, Sacred Places*. London: Routledge, pp. 32–43.

Courtright, P. 1987. Shrines. In Eliade, M. (ed.), *The Encyclopedia of Religion*. London: Macmillan, pp. 299–302.

Cremer, J. 1924. *Les Bobo (La Vie Sociale)*. Paris: Paul Geuthner.

Crone, P. 1987. *Meccan Trade and the Rise of Islam*. Princeton, N.J.: Princeton University Press.

Crook, J.H. 1995. Psychological Processes in Cultural and Genetic Co-evolution. In Jones, E. and Reynolds, E. (eds), *Survival and Religion*. Chichester: John Wiley, pp. 45–110.

D'Aquili, E. and Neuberg, A.B. 1999. *The Mystical Mind*. Minneapolis, Minn.: Fortress Press.

Davis, S. 1995. *The Archaeology of Animals*. London: Routledge.

Davis, W. 2001. Shamans as Botanical Researchers. In Narby, J. and Huxley, F. (eds), *Shamans Through Time*. London: Thames and Hudson, pp. 286–90.

Deacon, H.J. and Deacon, J. 1999. *Human Beginnings in South Africa*. Walnut Creek, Calif.: Altamira.

De Barros, P. 1990. Changing Paradigms, Goals and Methods in the Archaeology of Francophone West Africa. In Robertshaw, P. (ed.). *A History of African Archaeology*. London: James Currey, pp. 155–72.

De Heusch, L. 1985. *Sacrifice in Africa*. Manchester: Manchester University Press.

Delafosse, M. 1922. *Les Noirs de l'Afrique*. Paris: Payot.

Demarest, A.A. 1987. Archaeology and Religion. In Eliade, M. (ed.), *The Encyclopedia of Religion*. London: Macmillan, pp. 372–8.

Denny, F. 1985. Islamic Ritual. Perspectives and Theories. In Martin, R.C. (ed.), *Approaches to Islam in Religious Studies*. Tucson: University of Arizona Press, pp. 63–77.

D'Errico, F., Henshilwood, C. and Nilssen, P. 2001. An Engraved Bone Fragment from c.70,000-year-old MSA Levels at Blombos Cave, South Africa: Implications for the Origin of Symbolism and Language. *Antiquity* 75: 309–18.

Devereux, P. 2001. Did Ancient Shamanism Leave a Monumental Record on the Land as well as in Rock Art? In Wallis, R.J. and Lymer, K. (eds), *A Permeability of Boundaries*. BAR S936. Oxford: British Archaeological Reports, pp. 1–7.

Dietler, M. and Herbich, I. 1993. Living on Luo Time: Reckoning Sequence, Duration, History and Biography in a Rural African Society. *World Archaeology* 25: 248–60.

Dobres, M.-A. and Robb, J. 2000. *Agency in Archaeology*. London: Routledge.

Douglas, M. 1966. *Purity and Danger*. New York: Praeger.

Downes, J. and Pollard, T. (eds). 1999. *The Loved Body's Corruption: Archaeological Contributions to the Study of Human Mortality*. Glasgow: Cruithne Press.

Dowson, T. 2000. Why Queer Archaeology? An Introduction. *World Archaeology* 32: 161–5.

Drewal, H.J. 1997. Art or Accident: Yoruba Body Artists and Their Deity Ogun. In Barnes, S. (ed.), *Africa's Ogun. Old World and New*. Bloomington: Indiana University Press, pp. 235–60.

Drewal, H.J. and Mason, J. 1997. Ogun and Body/Mind Potentiality: Yoruba Scarification and Painting Traditions in Africa and the Americas. In Barnes, S. (ed.), *Africa's Ogun. Old World and New*. Bloomington: Indiana University Press, pp. 332–52.

Dronfield, J. 1996. Entering Alternative Realities: Cognition, Art and Architecture in Irish Passage-Tombs. *Cambridge Archaeological Journal* 6: 7–72.

Dumont, L. 1985. A Modified View of Our Origins: The Christian Beginnings of Modern Individualism. In Carrithers, M., Collins, S. and Lukes, S. (eds). *The Category of the Person*. Cambridge: Cambridge University Press, pp. 93–122.

Durkheim, E. 2001. *The Elementary Forms of Religious Life*. Oxford: Oxford University Press.

Durrans, B. 2000. (Not) Religion in Museums. In Paine, C. (ed.), *Godly Things. Museums, Objects and Religion*. Leicester: Leicester University Press, pp. 57–79.

Eaton, R.M. 1993. *The Rise of Islam and the Bengal Frontier, 1204–1760*. Berkeley: University of California Press.

Edmonds, M. 1999. *Ancestral Geographies of the Neolithic*. London: Routledge.

Eliade, M. 1958. *Patterns in Comparative Religion*. London: Sheed and Ward.

Eliade, M. 1959. *The Sacred and the Profane*. San Diego, Calif.: Harcourt.

Eliade, M. [1964] 1989. *Shamanism. Archaic Techniques of Ecstasy*. London: Penguin.

Eliade, M. 1969. *The Quest. History and Meaning in Religion*. Chicago, Ill.: University of Chicago Press.

Eliade, M. 1978a. *No Souvenirs*. London: Routledge.

Eliade, M. 1978b. Mythologies of Death. An Introduction. In Eliade, M., *Occultism, Witchcraft and Cultural Fashions*. London: University of Chicago Press, pp. 32–46.

Eliade, M. 1978c. Cultural Fashions and History of Religions. In Eliade, M., *Occultism, Witchcraft and Cultural Fashions*. London: University of Chicago Press, pp. 1–17.

Eliade, M. 1979. *A History of Religious Ideas. Volume 1. From the Stone Age to the Eleusinian Mysteries*. London: Collins.

Eriksen, T.H. 1995. *Small Places, Large Issues. An Introduction to Social and Cultural Anthropology*. London: Pluto Press.

Es-Sa'di, A. 1900. *Tarikh es-Soudan*. (O. Houdas, trans). Paris: Ernest Leroux.

Evans, C. 1999. Cognitive Maps and Narrative Trails: Fieldwork with the Tamu-Mai (Gurung) of Nepal. In Ucko, P. and Layton, R. (eds), *The Archaeology and Anthropology of Landscape*. London: Routledge, pp. 439–57.

Evans-Pritchard, E.E. 1965. *Theories of Primitive Religion*. Oxford: Oxford University Press.

Eyo, E. 1974. Odo Ogbe Street and Lafogido: Contrasting Archaeological Sites in Ile–Ife, Western Nigeria. *West African Journal of Archaeology* 4: 99–109.

Fagan, B. 1998. *From Black Land to Fifth Sun*. Reading, Mass.: Addison-Wesley.

Flannery, K.V. and Marcus, J. 1998. Cognitive Archaeology. In Whitley, D. (ed.), *Reader in Archaeological Theory*. London: Routledge, pp. 35–48.

Fleming, A. 1999. Phenomenology and the Megaliths of Wales: A Dreaming Too Far. *Oxford Journal of Archaeology* 18: 119–25.

Foucault, M. [1970] 2002. *The Order of Things*. London: Routledge.

Foucault, M. 1977. *Power/Knowledge*. London: The Harvester Press.

Foucault, M. 1985. *The Archaeology of Knowledge*. London: Tavistock.

Fowler, C. 2000. The Individual, The Subject and Archaeological Interpretation. In Holtorf, C. and Karlsson, H. (eds), *Philosophy and Archaeological Practice. Perspectives for the Twenty First Century*. Gothenburg: Bricoleur Press, pp. 107–33.

Frazer, J.G. 1936. *The Golden Bough (Adonis, Attis, Osiris, Vol. 2)*. London: Macmillan.

Freeman, L.G. and González Echegaray, J. 1981. El Juyo: A 14,000-Year-Old Sanctuary from Northern Spain. *History of Religions* 21: 1–19.

Frend, W.H.C. 1996. *The Archaeology of Early Christianity*. London: Geoffrey Chapman.

Fritz, J. 1978. Paleopsychology Today: Ideational Systems and Human Adaptation in Prehistory. In Redman, C. (ed.), *Social Archaeology: Beyond Subsistence and Dating*. New York: Academic Press, pp. 37–60.

Fuller, C.J. 1992. *The Camphor Flame*. Princeton, N.J.: Princeton University Press.

Gamble, C. 2001. *Archaeology. The Basics*. London: Routledge.

Gargett, R. 1989. Grave Shortcomings. *Current Anthropology* 30: 157–90.

Garlake, P. 1974. Excavations at Obalara's Land, Ife: An Interim Report. *West African Journal of Archaeology* 4: 111–48.

Garlake, P. 1978. *The Kingdoms of Africa*. Oxford: Elsevier Phaidon.

Garwood, P., Jennings, D., Skeates, R. and Toms, J. (eds). 1991. *Sacred and Profane*. Oxford: Oxbow Books.

Geertz, C. 1968. *Islam Observed*. New Haven, Conn.: Yale University Press.

Gerholm, T. 1988. On Ritual: A Postmodernist View. *Ethnos* 53: 190–203.

Gimbutas, M. 1989. *The Language of the Goddess*. London: Thames and Hudson.

Gimbutas, M. 1996. *The Goddesses and Gods of Old Europe*. London: Thames and Hudson.

Goldsmith, A.S., Garvie, S., Selin, D. and Smith, J. (eds). 1992. *Ancient Images. Ancient Thought. The Archaeology of Ideology*. Calgary: University of Calgary.

Goodison, L. and Morris, C. 1998. Introduction. In Goodison, L. and Morris, C. (eds), *Ancient Goddesses*. London: British Museum Press, pp. 6–21.

Gould, R. 1980. *Living Archaeology*. Cambridge: Cambridge University Press.

Grant, A. 1991. Economic or Symbolic? Animals and Ritual Behaviour. In Garwood, P. *et al.* (eds), *Sacred and Profane*, Oxford: Oxford Committee for Archaeology, pp. 109–14.

Green, M.J. 1998. The Time Lords: Ritual Calendars, Druids and the Sacred Year. In Gibson, A. and Simpson, D. (eds), *Prehistoric Ritual and Religion*. Stroud: Sutton, pp. 190–202.

Greene, K. 2002. *Archaeology: An Introduction*. London: Routledge.

Griaule, M. 1965. *Conversations with Ogotemeli. An Introduction to Dogon Religion*. London: Oxford University Press.

Griaule, M. and Dieterlen, G. 1965. *Le Renard Pâle*. Paris: Travaux et Mémoires de l'Institut d'Ethnologie.

Griaule, M. and Dieterlen, G. 1998. The Dogon. In Forde, D. (ed.), *African Worlds*. Oxford: James Currey, pp. 83–110.

Haaland, G. and Haaland, R. 1995. Who Speaks the Goddess's Language? Imagination and Method in Archaeological Research. *Norwegian Archaeological Review* 28: 105–21.

Hachlili, R. 1999. A Symbol of the Deity: Artistic Rendition of the 'Hand of God' in Ancient Jewish and Early Christian Art. In Insoll, T. (ed.), *Case Studies in Archaeology and World Religion*. BAR S755. Oxford: Archaeopress, pp. 59–70.

Hachlili, R. 2001. The Archaeology of Judaism. In Insoll, T. (ed.), *Archaeology and World Religion*, London: Routledge, pp. 96–122.

Hall, R.L. 1997. *An Archaeology of the Soul*. Urbana: University of Illinois Press.

Hamdun, S. and King, N. 1994. *Ibn Battuta in Black Africa*. Princeton, N.J.: Markus Wiener.

Hassan, F. 1997. Beyond the Surface: Comments on Hodder's Reflexive Excavation Methodology. *Antiquity* 71: 1020–5.

Hawkes, C. 1954. Archaeological Theory and Method: Some Suggestions from the Old World. *American Anthropology* 56: 153–68.

Hedges, J. [1984] 2000. *Tomb of the Eagles*. Oxford: John and Erica Hedges Ltd.

Hedges, K. 1992. Shamanistic Aspects of California Rock Art. In Bean, L.J. (ed.), *California Indian Shamanism*. Menlo Park, Calif.: Ballena Press, pp. 67–88.

Hegel, G.W.F. 1984. (P.C. Hodgson, ed.). *Lectures on the Philosophy of Religion. Volume 1, The Concept of Religion*. Berkeley: University of California Press.

Hegel, G.W.F. 1995. (P.C. Hodgson, ed.). *Lectures on the Philosophy of Religion. Volume 2, Determinate Religion*. Berkeley: University of California Press.

Hegel, G.W.F. 1998. (P.C. Hodgson, ed.). *Lectures on the Philosophy of Religion. Volume 3, The Consummate Religion*. Berkeley: University of California Press.

Heidegger, M. 1971. (A. Holstadter, trans.). *Poetry, Language, Thought*. London: Routledge and Kegan Paul.

Helvenston, P. and Bahn, P. 2002. *Desperately Seeking Trance Plants: Testing the 'Three Stages of Trance' Model*. New York: RJ Communications.

Hertz, R. 1973. The Hands. In Douglas, M. (ed.), *Rules and Meanings*. Harmondsworth: Penguin, pp. 118–24.

Hill, J.D. 1996. The Identification of Ritual Deposits of Animals. In Anderson, S. and Boyle, K. (eds), *Ritual Treatment of Human and Animal Remains*. Oxford: Oxbow, pp. 17–32.

Hinnells, J.R. (ed.). 1995. *The Penguin Dictionary of Religions*. London: Penguin.

# BIBLIOGRAPHY

Hoare, R. 1994. *The Turin Shroud is Genuine. The Irrefutable Evidence.* London: Souvenir Press.

Hodder, I. 1982. *The Present Past.* London: Batsford.

Hodder, I. 1988. *Reading the Past.* Cambridge: Cambridge University Press.

Hodder, I. 1990. *The Domestication of Europe.* Oxford: Blackwell.

Hodder, I. 1992. *Theory and Practice in Archaeology.* London: Routledge.

Hodder, I. (ed.). 1997a. *On the Surface: Catalhoyuk 1993–5.* Cambridge: McDonald Institute for Archaeological Research.

Hodder, I. 1997b. 'Always Momentary, Fluid and Flexible': Towards a Reflexive Excavation Methodology. *Antiquity* 71: 691–700.

Hodder, I. 1999. *The Archaeological Process. An Introduction.* Oxford: Blackwell.

Hodder, I. 2000. Developing a Reflexive Method in Archaeology. In Hodder, I. (ed.), *Towards Reflexive Method in Archaeology: The Example of Catalhoyuk.* Cambridge: McDonald Institute for Archaeological Research, pp. 3–14.

Hodder, I. 2001. Introduction. In Hodder, I. (ed.), *Archaeological Theory Today.* Oxford: Polity, pp. 1–13.

Hodgson, P.C. 1995. Editorial Introduction. In Hegel, G.W.F. *Lectures on the Philosophy of Religion. Volume 2, Determinate Religion.* Berkeley: University of California Press, pp. 1–90.

Holl, A. 1996. African History: Past, Present, and Future. In Schmidt, P. and Patterson, T. (eds), *Making Alternative Histories.* Santa Fe, N. Mex.: School of American Research Press, pp. 119–47.

Horia, V. 1969. The Forest as Mandala. In Kitagawa, J.M. and Long, C.H. (eds), *Myths and Symbols. Studies in Honour of Mircea Eliade.* Chicago: University of Chicago Press, pp. 387–95.

Horton, R. 1992. The Economy of Ife. *c.* AD 900–*c.* AD 1700. In Akinjogbin, I.A. (ed.), *The Cradle of a Race. Ife.* Port Harcourt, Nigeria: Sunray, pp. 122–47.

Houston, S. and Taube, K. 2000. An Archaeology of the Senses: Perception and Cultural Expression in Ancient Mesoamerica. *Cambridge Archaeological Journal* 10: 261–94.

Hubert, J. 1994. Sacred Beliefs and Beliefs of Sacredness. In Carmichael, D., Hubert, J., Reeves, B. and Schanche, A. (eds), *Sacred Sites, Sacred Places.* London: Routledge, pp. 9–19.

Hultkrantz, A. 1978. Ecological and Phenomenological Aspects of Shamanism. In Diószegi, V. and Hoppál, M. (eds), *Shamanism in Siberia.* Budapest: Akadémiai Kiadó, pp. 27–58.

# BIBLIOGRAPHY

Hurbon, L. 1995. *Voodoo. Truth and Fantasy.* London: Thames and Hudson.

Hutton, R. 2001. *Shamans. Siberian Spirituality and the Western Imagination.* London: Hambledon.

Ingold, T. 1986. *The Appropriation of Nature.* Manchester: Manchester University Press.

Ingold, T. 2000. *The Perception of the Environment.* London: Routledge.

Insoll, T. 1996. *Islam, Archaeology and History. Gao Region (Mali) Ca.AD 900–1250.* BAR S647. Oxford: Tempus Reparatum.

Insoll, T. 1999a. *The Archaeology of Islam.* Oxford: Blackwell.

Insoll, T. (ed.). 1999b. *Case Studies in Archaeology and World Religion. The Proceedings of the Cambridge Conference.* BAR S755. Oxford: Archaeopress.

Insoll, T. (with other contributions). 2000. *Urbanism, Archaeology and Trade. Further Observations on the Gao Region (Mali). The 1996 Fieldseason Results.* BAR S829. Oxford: British Archaeological Reports.

Insoll, T. (ed.). 2001a. *Archaeology and World Religion.* London: Routledge.

Insoll, T. 2001b. Introduction. The Archaeology of World Religion. In Insoll, T. (ed.), *Archaeology and World Religion.* London: Routledge, pp. 1–32.

Insoll, T. 2003. *The Archaeology of Islam in Sub-Saharan Africa.* Cambridge: Cambridge University Press.

Insoll, T. (ed.). 2004. *Trowelling Belief. The Proceedings of the Manchester Conference on Archaeology and Religion.* Oxford: Archaeopress.

Insoll, T. Forthcoming a. *Archaeology. The Conceptual Challenge.*

Insoll, T. Forthcoming b. *The Land of Enki in the Islamic Era. Pearls, Palms, and Religious Identity in Bahrain.* London: Kegan Paul.

James, E.O. 1957. *Prehistoric Religion.* London: Thames and Hudson.

James, W. 1988. *The Listening Ebony.* Oxford: Oxford University Press.

Jedrej, M.C. and Shaw, R. 1992. *Dreaming, Religion and Society in Africa.* Leiden: Brill.

Johanson, D. and Edgar, B. 2001. *From Lucy to Language.* London: Cassell.

Johnson, M. 1999. *Archaeological Theory. An Introduction.* Oxford: Blackwell.

Jones, A. 1998. Where Eagles Dare. *Journal of Material Culture* 3: 301–24.

Jones, S. 1997. *The Archaeology of Ethnicity.* London: Routledge.

Kehoe, A. 2000. *Shamans and Religion*. Prospect Heights, Ill.: Waveland Press.

Kemp, B. 1995. How Religious were the Ancient Egyptians? *Cambridge Archaeological Journal* 5: 25–54.

Koloss, H.-J. n.d. Congo. In Koloss, H.-J. (ed.), *Africa. Art and Culture*. Berlin: Prestel, pp. 124–6.

Kristiansen, K. 1984. Ideology and Material Culture: An Archaeological Perspective. In Spriggs, M. (ed.), *Marxist Perspectives in Archaeology*. Cambridge: Cambridge University Press, pp. 72–100.

Kus, S. 1984. The Spirit and its Burden: Archaeology and Symbolic Activity. In Spriggs, M. (ed.), *Marxist Perspectives in Archaeology*. Cambridge: Cambridge University Press, pp. 101–7.

Lad, G. 1983. *Mahabharata and Archaeological Evidence*. Poona: Deccan College.

La Fontaine, J.S. 1985. Person and Individual. Some Anthropological Reflections. In Carrithers, M., Collins, S. and Lukes, S. (eds) *The Category of the Person*. Cambridge: Cambridge University Press, pp. 123–40.

Lane, P. 2001. The Archaeology of Christianity in Global Perspective. In Insoll, T. (ed.), *Archaeology and World Religion*. London: Routledge, pp. 148–81.

Latham, J.E. 1987. Food. In Eliade, M. (ed.), *The Encyclopedia of Religion*. London: Macmillan, pp. 387–93.

Layton, R. and Ucko, P. 1999. Introduction. In Ucko, P. and Layton, R. (eds), *The Archaeology and Anthropology of Landscape*. London: Routledge, pp. 1–20.

Le Moal, G. 1980. *Les Bobo. Nature et Fonction des Masques*. Paris: ORSTOM.

Lévi-Strauss, C. 1973. *Tristes Tropiques*. Harmondsworth: Penguin.

Lévi-Strauss, C. 1978. *Structural Anthropology 2*. Harmondsworth: Penguin.

Lévi-Strauss, C. [1962] 1991. *Totemism*. London: Merlin Press.

Lévi-Strauss, C. [1964] 1994. *The Raw and the Cooked*. London: Pimlico.

Levtzion, N. 1986. Rural and Urban Islam in West Africa. An Introductory Essay. *Asian and African Studies* 20: 7–26.

Lewis, G. 1980. *Day of Shining Red*. Cambridge: Cambridge University Press.

Lewis-Williams, D. 2002. *The Mind in the Cave*. London: Thames and Hudson.

Lissner, I. 1961. *Man, God and Magic*. London: Jonathan Cape.

Lowenstein, T. 1993. *Ancient Land: Sacred Whale. The Inuit Hunt and its Rituals*. London: Bloomsbury.

Lyotard, J.F. 1984. *The Postmodern Condition: A Report on Knowledge*. Manchester: Manchester University Press.

McBrearty, S. and Brooks, A.S. 2000. The Revolution that Wasn't: A New Interpretation of the Origin of Modern Human Behaviour. *Journal of Human Evolution* 39: 453–563.

McCauley, R.N. and Lawson, E.T. 2002. *Bringing Ritual to Mind. Psychological Foundations of Cultural Forms*. Cambridge: Cambridge University Press.

MacDonald, K. 1995. Why Chickens? The Centrality of the Domestic Fowl in West African Ritual and Magic. In Ryan, K. and Crabtree, P.J. (eds), *The Symbolic Role of Animals in Archaeology*. Philadelphia: University of Pennsylvania Museum of Archaeology and Anthropology, pp. 51–6.

McGrath, A.E. 1993. *Reformation Thought. An Introduction*. Oxford: Blackwell.

McGuire, R. 1992. *A Marxist Archaeology*. San Diego, Calif.: Academic Press.

McIntosh, R.J. and McIntosh, S.K. 1979. Terracotta Statuettes from Mali. *African Arts* 12(2): 51–3.

Mandal, D. 1993. *Ayodhya. Archaeology after Demolition*. London: Sangam Books.

Maringer, J. 1960. *The Gods of Prehistoric Man*. London: Weidenfeld and Nicolson.

Maringer, J. 1977. Priests and Priestesses in Prehistoric Europe. *History of Religions* 17: 101–20.

Maringer, J. 1979. Adorants in Prehistoric Art. *Numen* 26: 215–30.

Marx, K. and Engels, F. 1972. *On Religion*. Moscow: Progress Publishers.

Mauny, R. 1961. *Tableau Géographique de l'Ouest Africain au Moyen Age*. Dakar: Institut Français de l'Afrique Noire.

Mautner, T. 1997. *The Penguin Dictionary of Philosophy*. London: Penguin.

Mbiti, J.S. 1991. *Introduction to African Religion*. Oxford: Heinemann.

Mellaart, J. 1964. A Neolithic City in Turkey. *Scientific American* (April): 1–11.

Mellaart, J. 1967. *Catal Huyuk: A Neolithic Town in Anatolia*. London: Thames and Hudson.

Mellars, P. 1989. Major Issues in the Emergence of Modern Humans. *Current Anthropology* 30: 349–85.

Mellars, P. 1996. *The Neanderthal Legacy*. Princeton, N.J.: Princeton University Press.

Menski, W. 2002. Review of Weinberger-Thomas, C. 'Ashes of Immortality. Widow-Burning in India'. *Journal of the Royal Asiatic Society* 12: 396–8.

Merkur, D. 1991. *Powers which we do not Know*. Moscow, Ida.: University of Idaho Press.

Merleau-Ponty, M. [1962] 2003. *Phenomenology of Perception*. London: Routledge.

Merrifield, R. 1987. *The Archaeology of Ritual and Magic*. London: Batsford.

Meskell, L. 1995. Goddesses, Gimbutas and 'New Age' Archaeology. *Antiquity* 69: 74–86.

Meskell, L. 1998. Twin Peaks. The Archaeologies of Catalhöyük. In Goodison, L. and Morris, C. (eds), *Ancient Goddesses*. London: British Museum Press, pp. 46–62.

Meslin, M. 1985. From the History of Religions to Religious Anthropology: A Necessary Reappraisal. In Kitagawa, J. (ed.), *The History of Religions. Retrospect and Prospect*. London: Collier Macmillan, pp. 31–52.

Métraux, A. 1989. *Voodoo in Haiti*. New York: Schocken Books.

Miller, D. and Tilley, C. 1984. Ideology, Power and Prehistory: An Introduction. In Miller, D. and Tilley, C. (eds), *Ideology, Power and Prehistory*. Cambridge: Cambridge University Press, pp. 1–15.

Mithen, S. 1998. *The Prehistory of the Mind*. London: Phoenix.

Moran, D. 2000. *Introduction to Phenomenology*. London: Routledge.

Morris, B. 1987. *Anthropological Studies of Religion*. Cambridge: Cambridge University Press.

Morris, B. 1994. *Anthropology of the Self*. London: Pluto Press.

Mudimbe, V.W. 1988. *The Invention of Africa*. Bloomington: Indiana University Press.

Murray, T. (ed.). 1999. *Time and Archaeology*. London: Routledge.

Myers, F.R. 1991. *Pintupi Country, Pintupi Self*. Berkeley: University of California Press.

Narby, J. and Huxley, F. (eds). 2001. *Shamans Through Time*. London: Thames and Hudson.

Narr, K.J. 1964. Approaches to the Religion of Early Palaeolithic Man. *History of Religions* 4: 1–22.

Nash, R.J. 1997. Archetypal Landscapes and the Interpretation of Meaning. *Cambridge Archaeological Journal* 7: 57–69.

Needham, R. 1972. *Belief, Language and Experience*. Oxford: Blackwell.

Needham, R. 1975. Polythetic Classification. *Man* 10: 349–69.

Norton, J. 1992. Ridge Walkers of North-Western California: Paths Toward Spiritual Balance. In Bean, L.J. (ed.), *California Indian Shamanism*. Menlo Park, Calif.: Ballena Press, pp. 227–36.

Obayemi, A.M. 1992. The Phenomenon of Oduduwa in Ife History. In Akinjogbin, I.A. (ed.), *The Cradle of a Race. Ife*. Port Harcourt, Nigeria: Sunray, pp. 62–76.

Oestigaard, T. 1999. Cremations as Transformations: When the Dual Cremation Hypothesis was Cremated and Carried away in Urns. *European Journal of Archaeology* 2: 345–64.

Oestigaard, T. 2000a. Sacrifices of Raw, Cooked and Burnt Humans. *Norwegian Archaeological Review* 33: 41–58.

Oestigaard, T. 2000b. *The Deceased's Life Cycle Rituals in Nepal*. BAR S853. Oxford: British Archaeological Reports.

Oestigaard, T. 2003. *An Archaeology of Hell*. Gothenburg: Bricoleur Press.

Ogundiran, A.O. 2002. Filling a Gap in the Ife-Benin Interaction Field (13th–16th Centuries AD): Excavations in Iloyi Settlement, Ijesaland. *African Archaeological Review* 19: 27–60.

Olaniyan, R.A. and Akinjogbin, I.A. 1992. Sources of the History of Ife. In Akinjogbin, I.A. (ed.), *The Cradle of a Race. Ife*. Port Harcourt, Nigeria: Sunray, pp. 39–50.

Olomola, I. 1992. Ife before Oduduwa. In Akinjogbin, I.A. (ed.), *The Cradle of a Race. Ife*. Port Harcourt, Nigeria: Sunray, pp. 51–61.

Olupona, J.K. 1993. The Study of Yoruba Religious Tradition in Historical Perspective. *Numen* 40: 240–73.

Ortiz, R. 1997. Ogum and the Umbandista Religion. In Barnes, S. (ed.), *Africa's Ogun. Old World and New*. Bloomington: Indiana University Press, pp. 90–102.

O'Shea, J. 1984. *Mortuary Variability. An Archaeological Investigation*. New York: Academic Press.

Otto, R. 1950. *The Idea of the Holy*. Oxford: Oxford University Press.

Ovsyannikov, O.V. and Terebikhin, N.M. 1994. Sacred Space in the Culture of the Arctic Regions. In Carmichael, D., Hubert, J., Reeves, B. and Schanche, A. (eds), *Sacred Sites, Sacred Places*. London: Routledge, pp. 44–81.

Paden, W. 1994. *Religious Worlds*. Boston, Mass.: Beacon Press.

Parker Pearson, M. 1982. Mortuary Practices, Society and Ideology: An Ethnoarchaeological Study. In Hodder, I. (ed.), *Symbolic and Structural Archaeology*. Cambridge: Cambridge University Press, pp. 99–113.

Parker Pearson, M. 1984. Social Change, Ideology and the Archaeo-logical Record. In Spriggs, M. (ed.), *Marxist Perspectives in Archaeology*. Cambridge: Cambridge University Press, pp. 59–71.

Parker Pearson, M. 1999. *The Archaeology of Death and Burial*. Stroud: Sutton Publishing.

Parker Pearson, M. 2001. Death, Being and Time. The Historical Con-text of the World Religions. In Insoll, T. (ed.), *Archaeology and World Religion*. London: Routledge, pp. 203–19.

Peake, M. 1978. *Titus Groan*. Harmondsworth: Penguin.

Pearson, J.L. 2002. *Shamanism and the Ancient Mind*. Walnut Creek, Calif.: Altamira.

Pemberton, J. 1997. The Dreadful God and the Divine King. In Barnes, S. (ed.), *Africa's Ogun. Old World and New*. Bloomington: Indiana University Press, pp. 105–46.

Peters, F.H. 2000. Neurophenomenology. *Method and Theory in the Study of Religion* 12: 379–415.

Pettigrew, J. and Tamu, Y. 1999. The Kohla Project: Studying the Past with the Tamu-Mai. *Studies in Nepali History and Society* 4: 327–64.

Picknett, L. and Prince, C. 1994. *Turin Shroud. In Whose Image? The Shocking Truth Unveiled*. London: Bloomsbury Publishers.

Piggott, S. 1985. *William Stukeley. An Eighteenth-Century Antiquary*. London: Thames and Hudson.

Poynor, R. 1987–88. Ako Figures of Owo and Second Burials in Southern Nigeria. *African Arts* 21(1): 62–3, 81–7.

Price, N.S. 2001. An Archaeology of Altered States: Shamanism and Material Culture Studies. In Price, N. (ed.), *The Archaeology of Shamanism*. London: Routledge, pp. 3–16.

Radford, C.A.R. 1971. Christian Origins in Britain. *Medieval Archaeology* 15: 1–12.

Ranger, T. 1991. African Traditional Religions. In Sutherland, S. and Clarke, P. (eds). *The Study of Religion, Traditional and New Religion*. London: Routledge, pp. 106–14.

Rao, N. 1999. Ayodhya and the Ethics of Archaeology. (In) Insoll, T. (ed.), *Case Studies in Archaeology and World Religion*. Oxford: Archaeo-press, pp. 44–7.

Reitz, E.J. and Wing, E.S. 1999. *Zooarchaeology*. Cambridge: Cambridge University Press.

Renfrew, C. 1985. *The Archaeology of Cult*. London: Thames and Hudson.

Renfrew, C. 1989. *Archaeology and Language*. London: Penguin.

Renfrew, C. 1994a. The Archaeology of Religion. In Renfrew, C. and Zubrow, E. (eds), *The Ancient Mind*. Cambridge: Cambridge University Press, pp. 47–54.

Renfrew, C. 1994b. Towards a Cognitive Archaeology. In Renfrew, C. and Zubrow, E. (eds), *The Ancient Mind*. Cambridge: Cambridge University Press, pp. 3–12.

Renfrew, C. and Bahn, P. 2000. *Archaeology. Theories, Methods, and Practice*. London: Thames and Hudson.

Ricoeur, P. 1985. The History of Religions and the Phenomenology of Time Conciousness. In Kitagawa, J. (ed.), *The History of Religions. Retrospect and Prospect*. London: Collier Macmillan, pp. 13–30.

Ries, J. 1994. *The Origins of Religions*. Grand Rapids, Mich.: William B. Eerdmans.

Rodwell, W. 1989. *The Archaeology of Religious Places. Churches and Cemeteries in Britain*. Philadelphia: University of Pennsylvania Press.

Rose, D.B. 1992. *Dingo Makes Us Human*. Cambridge: Cambridge University Press.

Rouch, J. 1953. *Contribution à l'Histoire des Songhay*. Dakar: Institut Français de l'Afrique Noire.

Ruggles, C. 1998. *Astronomy in Prehistoric Britain and Ireland*. New Haven, Conn.: Yale University Press.

Saliba, J.A. 1976. *'Homo Religiosus' in Mircea Eliade*. Leiden: Brill.

Scarre, C. 1994. The Meaning of Death: Funerary Beliefs and the Prehistorian. In Renfrew, C. and Zubrow, E. (eds), *The Ancient Mind*. Cambridge: Cambridge University Press, pp. 75–82.

Scruton, R. 2002. *A Short History of Modern Philosophy*. London: Routledge.

Shanks, M. and Tilley, C. 1982. Ideology, Symbolic Power and Ritual Communication. A Reinterpretation of Neolithic Mortuary Remains. In Hodder, I. (ed.), *Symbolic and Structural Archaeology*. Cambridge: Cambridge University Press, pp. 129–54.

Shanks, M. and Tilley, C. 1992. *Re-Constructing Archaeology. Theory and Practice*. London: Routledge.

Sharpe, E.J. 1986. *Comparative Religion. A History*. London: Duckworth.

Shaw, J. 1999. Buddhist Landscapes and Monastic Planning: The Elements of Intervisibility, Surveillance and the Protection of Relics. In Insoll, T. (ed.), *Case Studies in Archaeology and World Religion*. BAR S755. Oxford: Archaeopress, pp. 5–17.

Shaw, R. 1990. The Invention of 'African Traditional Religion'. *Religion* 20: 339–53.

Shaw, R. and Stewart, C. 1994. Introduction: Problematizing Syncretism. In Stewart, C. and Shaw, S. (eds), *Syncretism/Anti Syncretism. The Politics of Religious Synthesis*. London: Routledge, pp. 1–26.

Silberman, N.A. 1998. Whose Game is it Anyway? The Political and Social Transformations of American Biblical Archaeology. In Meskell, L. (ed.), *Archaeology Under Fire*. London: Routledge, pp. 175–88.

Simoons, F.J. 1994. *Eat Not This Flesh*. Madison: University of Wisconsin Press.

Smith, I. 1965. *Windmill Hill and Avebury. Exacavations by Alexander Keiller, 1925–1939*. Oxford: Clarendon Press.

Smith, J.Z. 1980. The Bare Facts of Ritual. *History of Religions* 20: 112–27.

Solecki, R. 1971. *Shanidar – The First Flower People*. New York: Knopf.

Solomon, A. 1997. The Myth of Ritual Origins? Ethnography, Mythology and Interpretation of San Rock Art. *South African Archaeological Bulletin* 52: 3–13.

Solomon, A. 2000. On Different Approaches to San Rock Art. *South African Archaeological Bulletin* 55: 77–8.

Sommers, J.D. 1999. The Shanidar IV 'Flower Burial': A Re-Evaluation of Neanderthal Burial Ritual. *Cambridge Archaeological Journal* 9: 127–37.

Strassburg, J. 2000. *Shamanic Shadows: One Hundred Generations of Undead Subversion in Southern Scandinavia, 7,000–4,000 BC*. Stockholm: University of Stockholm.

Strenski, I. (ed.). 1992. *Malinowski and the Work of Myth*. Princeton, N.J.: Princeton University Press.

Stringer, C. and Gamble, C. 1993. *In Search of the Neanderthals*. London: Thames and Hudson.

Swidler, N., Dongoske, K., Anyon, R. and Downer, A. (eds). 1997. *Native Americans and Archaeologists: Stepping Stones to Common Ground*. Walnut Creek, Calif.: Altamira.

Tarlow, S. 2000. Emotion in Archaeology. *Current Anthropology* 41: 713–46.

Taylor, T. 2002. *The Buried Soul. How Humans Invented Death*. London: Fourth Estate.

Theodoratus, D.J. and LaPena, F. 1994. Wintu Sacred Geography of Northern California. In Carmichael, D., Hubert, J., Reeves, B. and Schanche, A. (eds), *Sacred Sites, Sacred Places*. London: Routledge, pp. 20–31.

Thomas, D.H. 1998. *Archaeology*. New York: Harcourt Brace.

Thomas, J. 1988. The Social Significance of Cotswold–Severn Burial Practices. *Man* 23: 540–59.

Thomas, J. 1996. *Time, Culture and Identity*. London: Routledge.

Thomas, J. (ed.). 2000. *Interpretive Archaeology. A Reader*. London: Leicester University Press.

Thomas, J. 2001. Archaeologies of Place and Landscape. In Hodder, I. (ed.), *Archaeological Theory Today*. Oxford: Polity, pp. 165–86.

Tilley, C. 1994. *A Phenomenology of Landscape*. Oxford: Berg.

Trigger, B. 1989. *A History of Archaeological Thought*. Cambridge: Cambridge University Press.

Tringham, R. and Conkey, M. 1998. Rethinking Figurines. In Goodison, L. and Morris, C. (eds), *Ancient Goddesses*. London: British Museum Press, pp. 22–45.

Tylden-Wright, D. 1991. *John Aubrey. A Life*. London: HarperCollins.

Tylor, E.B. 1929. *Primitive Culture*. 2 Vols. London: John Murray.

Tylor, E.B. 1958. *Religion in Primitive Culture*. New York: Harper and Row.

Ucko, P. 1969. Ethnography and the Archaeological Interpretation of Funerary Remains. *World Archaeology* 1: 262–90.

Ucko, P. 2001. Unprovenanced Material Culture and Freud's Collection of Antiquities. *Journal of Material Culture* 6: 269–322.

Unger, M.F. 1962. *Archaeology and the New Testament*. Grand Rapids, Mich.: Zondervan.

Van Beek, W. 1988. Functions of Sculpture in Dogon Religion. *African Arts* 21(4): 58–65.

Van Beek, W. 1991. Dogon Restudied. *Current Anthropology* 32: 139–67.

Vitebsky, P. 1995. *The Shaman*. London: Little, Brown and Co.

Von Stietencron, H. 1989. Hinduism: On the Proper Use of a Deceptive Term. In Southeimer, G.D. and Kulke, H. (eds), *Hinduism Reconsidered*. New Delhi: Manohar, pp. 11–27.

Wadley, L. 2001. What is Cultural Modernity? A General View and South African Perspective from Rose Cottage Cave. *Cambridge Archaeological Journal* 11: 201–21.

Wallis, R.J. 2001. Waking Ancestor Spirits: Neo-Shamanic Engagements with Archaeology. In Price, N. (ed.), *The Archaeology of Shamanism*. London: Routledge, pp. 213–30.

Wallis, R.J. and Lymer, K. 2001. Introduction. In Wallis, R.J. and Lymer, K. (eds), *A Permeability of Boundaries*. Oxford: British Archaeological Reports. BAR S936, pp. xiii–xviii.

Walshe, J.G. and Warrier, S. 1997. *Dates and Meanings of Religious and Other Festivals*. Chippenham: Foulsham.

Wansbrough, J. 1977. *Quranic Studies: Sources and Methods of Scriptural Interpretation*. Oxford: Oxford University Press.

Watkins, J. 2000. *Indigenous Archaeology*. Walnut Creek, Calif.: Altamira.

Weber, M. 1963. *The Sociology of Religion*. Boston, Mass.: Beacon Press.

Wenke, R. 1990. *Patterns in Prehistory*. Oxford: Oxford University Press.

White Deer, G. 1998. Return of the Sacred. Spirituality and the Scientific Imperative. In Whitley, D. (ed.), *Reader in Archaeological Theory*. London: Routledge, pp. 331–7.

Whitelam, K.W. 1996. *The Invention of Ancient Israel*. London: Routledge.

Whitley, D. 1998. New Approaches to Old Problems. In Whitley, D. (ed.), *Reader in Archaeological Theory*. London: Routledge, pp. 1–28.

Whitley, J. 2002. Too Many Ancestors. *Antiquity* 76: 119–26.

Willett, F. 1959. Bronze and Terra-Cotta Sculptures from Ita Yemoo, Ife. *South African Archaeological Bulletin* 14: 135–7.

Willett, F. 1970. Excavations at Ita Yemoo, Nigeria. In Anon, *Actes du VIIe Congrès International des Sciences Préhistoriques et Protohistoriques, Prague, 1966*. Prague: Institut d'Archéologie Tchécoslavaque des Sciences à Prague.

Winkelman, M. 2002. Shamanism and Cognitive Evolution. *Cambridge Archaeological Journal* 12: 71–101.

Wittgenstein, L. (G.M. Anscombe, trans.). 1953. *Philosophical Investigations*. Oxford: Blackwell.

Wylie, A. 1985. The Reaction against Analogy. *Advances in Archaeological Method and Theory* 8: 63–111.

Yahya, H. 2001. *Perished Nations*. London: Ta-Ha Publishers.

Yamauchi, E.M. 1972. *The Stones and the Scriptures*. New York: Holman.

Young, D.E. and Goulet, J.-G. 1994. Introduction. In Young, D.E. and Goulet, J.-G. (eds), *Being Changed by Cross-Cultural Encounters. The Anthropology of Extraordinary Experience*. Ontario: Broadview Press, pp. 7–13.

Zahan, D. 1974. *The Bambara*. Leiden: Brill.

Zeusse, E.M. 1987. Ritual. In Eliade, M. (ed.), *The Encyclopedia of Religion. Volume 12*. London: Macmillan, pp. 405–22.

Zeusse, E.M. 1991. Perseverance and Transmutation in African Traditional Religions. In Olupone, J.K. (ed.), *African Traditional Religions in Contemporary Society*. New York: Paragon House, pp. 167–84.

Zvelebil, M. 1997. Hunter-Gatherer Ritual Landscapes: Spatial Organisation, Social Structure and Ideology among Hunter-Gatherers of
Northern Europe and Western Siberia. *Analecta Praehistorica Leidensia*
29: 33–50.

# INDEX

Africa (*see also* entries for
  individual countries): MSA 26,
  32; early man 27, 30;
  ethnography 43; Jihads 79;
  epistemological regions 127;
  traditional religions 139, 145
agency, individual 2, 14, 77, 79,
  153
agnosticism 21
agriculture: origins of 47, 66;
  and seasonality 45, 131; and
  religion 53, 66; and fertility
  45; and Goddess cults 57;
  Dogon 120
Ainu 54
Akhenaten 17
altars 106, 118
Amazonian Rainforest 87
analogy, use of (*see also*
  ethnography, Eliade, Foucault,
  Frazer, Hodder, Narr, Tylor,
  Ucko): and prehistoric religion
  45, 53, 54, 55, 113–116; and
  death 67–8; post-processual
  approach 77; rock art 94;
  shamanism 95; West African
  religion 101, 111, 113–16
ancestors: as custodians 45; cults
  65, 66, 114, 135; ancestral

past 84, 86, 98, 121; in Nepal
  98; in West Africa 103, 114,
  121, 132–3, 135; in Orkney
  114, 121; Australian
  aboriginal 130
animals 48, 74
animism (*see also* Tyler): as
  primal religion 29, 32, 44, 45;
  identification of 59, 73, 103;
  in West Africa 103, 139;
  misuse and definition of 139,
  140, 155
anthropology: and religion 34–5,
  38, 75; and archaeology 47,
  75; and shamanism 58; and
  analogy 115; and myth 128
anthropomorphism 30, 43, 73
antiquarianism 42–6
archaeoastronomy 129
archaeobotany 66
art: development of 26, 28;
  Neanderthal 29; rock art 58,
  93, 94, 142; and art history
  59; ancient near Eastern,
  Jewish and Christian 59–60; at
  Çatal Hüyük 82; West African
  104, 107, 110, 133–4;
  prehistoric European 126
atheism 21, 43, 147

symbols/symbolism: origins of 23, 24, 25, 32, 33; interpretation of 34, 49, 56; and archaeology 47, 73, 77; and art history 59; West African 123, 137, 138
syncretism 101, 128, 131–9, 145, 149

taboo 71, 75–6
Tarlow, S. 112
technology 22, 118, 121, 127, 151
Tell el-Amarna 17
temples 17, 22, 51, 62, 74
Teshik Tash 28
theology 4, 21
Thomas, J. 79, 80, 88, 91
'three age system' 44
Tilley, C. 85, 87–8
time 79, 101, 124, 128, 129–31, 137, 151–2
tombs (see also burials) 58, 66, 67, 88, 113–14, 154
totemism 29, 30, 32, 43, 140, 155
traditional religions 46, 136: definition of 5, 8, 9, 119, 139, 155; contemporary 97–100; West African 101, 102, 119, 139, 145, 149
trees 91, 103, 105–6
Trobriand Islands 127
Tungus 54, 140
Turin Shroud 61–2
Turkey 50, 57
Tylor, E. 6, 44, 45

United Kingdom 52, 69, 73, 86, 88, 111

Upper Palaeolithic: and religion 5, 23, 30, 32, 56, 65, 143; numinous in 20; revolution 26; material culture 31; art 93, 94, 142
United States of America 48, 49, 50, 71, 97–100, 103, 142
Uzbekistan 28

Vico, G. 93
Voudou 102

Wallis, R. 63–4, 99
Weber, M. 36
Wenke, R. 2, 3
West Africa (see also entries for individual countries): religion in 4, 101–10, 119, 128, 132, 138; chicken in 74
Whitley, J. 66
Willett, F. 109–10
witchcraft 34
Wittgenstein, L. 144
world religions (see also Buddhism, Christianity, Hinduism, Islam and Judaism): and archaeology 1, 5, 46, 59, 63; definition of 8; and faith 21; and anthropology 34; in West Africa 119; and traditional religion 119, 136, 155; and Hinduism 143

Yoruba: philosophy 79; religion 101–10, 116–19, 125, 128, 139, 140; ethnography 113, 115, 116–19

Zvelebil, M. 126–7